The Clean Cook:
The Virgin Diet for Vegans, Vegetarians, and Pescetarians

100 Delicious Allergen-Free (Soy-Free, Corn-Free, Egg-Free, Dairy-Free, Sugar-Free, Peanut-Free, and Gluten-Free) Recipes

D0711978

by

Rachelle Street

DISCLAIMER

This cookbook is for educational purposes. The author of this cookbook is not responsible in any manner whatsoever for any adverse effects arising directly or indirectly as a result of the information or recipes provided in this book. Read and use the information contained in this publication at your own risk.

If you have special dietary needs, it is important to consult with your physician. Neither this diet nor any other diet program should be followed without first consulting a health-care professional. If you have special dietary conditions requiring attention, you should consult with your health-care professional regularly regarding possible modification of the program contained in this book.

CONTENTS

A NOTE ON NUTRITIONAL INFORMATION

All of the nutritional information provided in this book, such as calorie count, protein, fiber, fat content, etc. was obtained using the online food tracking application CRON-O-Meter (©Copyright 2011-2014, BigCrunch Consulting, Ltd.). I tried to be as accurate as possible in estimating portion sizes and entering sizes and weights for the ingredients in each recipe. Variations in the sizes of fruits and vegetables used in the recipes will cause slight nutritional count variations, but what is provided is a fairly accurate estimate.

1
INTRODUCTION

I grew up eating processed foods from boxes and cans. My siblings and I were classic latch-key kids with a sometimes-single mother working one or two jobs, depending on her financial situation. We received food stamps and boxes of food from church food drives. My mother had neither the time nor the energy to produce meals from scratch. We also lived in the middle of small-town Wisconsin; even today one can be hard-pressed to find fresh lettuce in the tiny local grocery stores. During the summers we were really on our own, cooking our own meals while our mother was at work. A regular day was filled with sugary cereals, store-brand macaroni-and-cheese, and hot dogs.

I feel very fortunate now to have the luxury of time and resources to eat a clean, healthy diet that is rich in all the foods I didn't have access to as a child. At the age of eighteen I became a vegetarian and realized I needed to teach myself how to cook. I bought a comprehensive cookbook titled *1000 Vegetarian Recipes,* by Carol Gelles, and spent a year methodically cooking my way through the massive tome, making notes as I went along so I learned what I liked and how to alter the recipes to improve them.

Becoming a Vegetarian

I became a vegetarian for health reasons. I was working three jobs to pay for college and I was always tired from the massive amounts of coffee and junk food I was consuming. Let me make it clear that it is quite easy to be an unhealthy vegetarian—french fries, potato chips, and pizza are all vegetarian foods. But I gave up the coffee, and discovered foods like spinach, tomatoes, tofu, and avocados. As I learned more about being a vegetarian, I realized that it was a much better choice for the environment as well as my body. The statistics are staggering:

- It takes 23 gallons of water to produce a pound of tomatoes; it takes 5214 gallons of water to produce a pound of beef.
- One acre of land can produce 20,000 pounds of potatoes; one acre of land can produce 165 pounds of beef.
- It takes one pound of grain to make one pound of bread; it takes 20 pounds of grain to make one pound of beef.
- The U.S. cattle industry produces 158 million tons of waste a year and livestock production is the #1 cause of water pollution in the U.S.
- The countries with diets highest in animal products are also the countries with the highest rates of cancer, heart disease, diabetes, and osteoporosis.

It is facts like these that continue to fuel my passion for vegetarianism. However, I never pressure meat-eaters to give up their meat—I respect a person's right to chose what they put in their bodies.

I am not a vegan. My grandparents were dairy farmers and even to this day I occasionally indulge in cheese. I can give up milk, yogurt, butter, but brie is my kryptonite! I always regret it the next day, but find it nearly impossible to resist. I also love my wool sweaters and own leather shoes. I enjoy honey in my tea. I admire vegans—they are stronger than I am!

A few years ago I realized that my soy-heavy diet was not working for me. I was experience a large amount of digestive issues. Truthfully, I've had digestive issues my entire life, and the soy seemed to be exacerbating it. I couldn't live on beans alone, so I slowly starting reintroducing fish into my diet. I now eat fish once or twice a week. I know quite a few vegetarians who have returned to fish for the same soy-based reasons as me. Trust me when I say I am not pushing seafood on anyone! I've tucked the seafood recipes in the back so you can completely ignore them if you like.

An added bonus of being a vegetarian is the savings on groceries. Meat is expensive! Especially if you want to eat only grass-fed, antibiotic-free, non-GMO meats. I, like many, try to eat organic and non-GMO as much as possible. However, sometimes buying organic means paying as much as triple for my fruits and vegetables. The Environmental Working Group puts out an annual list of the "Dirty Dozen," the fruits and vegetables that contain the most pesticide residues, and the "Clean Fifteen," the fruits and vegetables that are the least contaminated and, ergo, you can save you money when purchasing those items. At the time of this publication, the Dirty Dozen Plus were:

- Apples
- Celery
- Cherry tomatoes
- Cucumbers
- Grapes
- Hot peppers
- Imported nectarines
- Peaches
- Potatoes
- Spinach
- Strawberries
- Sweet bell peppers (This one kills me—organic red bell peppers cost three times the price of non-organic!)
- Kale and collard greens
- Summer squash and zucchini

Don't despair, however, as you can save your pennies by buying the following Clean Fifteen items without an organic label:

- Asparagus
- Avocados
- Cabbage
- Cantaloupe

- Sweet Corn (if you can find it non-GMO!)
- Eggplant
- Grapefruit
- Kiwi
- Mangos
- Mushrooms
- Onions
- Papayas
- Pineapples
- Frozen sweet peas
- Sweet potatoes

Another money-saving tip is to buy fruit and vegetables frozen whenever possible. They're frozen at the peak of freshness and won't spoil. I use frozen spinach for soups and stir fries, and frozen organic fruit is much cheaper than the fresh variety. You don't need fresh blueberries for that smoothie!

A good way to pinch pennies is to buy your legumes dried. Sure, you have to soak them overnight and then boil them for an hour, but a single 1-pound bag of black beans costs $2 and has 12 servings. A can of black beans also costs $2, but has only three servings. You're spending four times as much for canned as opposed to dried. Of course, if time is of the essence and you don't like too much prepping, go with what works best for you.

One last piece of grocery buying advice is to buy bouillon stock instead of broth. I use vegetable bouillon whenever I make anything dried—rice, beans, lentils—to give it extra flavor. It would be very expensive to use store-bought pints of broth. Bouillon cubes, however, can contain a lot of salt and saturated fats. I love Better than Bouillon—a concentrated vegetable base.

Discovering the Virgin Diet

After years of trying to figure out my digestive issues, I was becoming increasingly frustrated. I tried the specific-carbohydrate diet, the South Beach diet, the Martha's Vineyard diet, juice cleanses; I had test upon test performed by doctors to no avail. I was diagnosed with irritable bowel syndrome—a meaningless catch-all diagnosis that doctors give when they don't know what's wrong nor how to fix it. I had sleepless nights when I was filled with nausea. I was incredibly sensitive to smells. I was a monster to travel with—if I didn't eat constantly I would go into a massive hunger rage. Then I decided to give the Virgin Diet a go. I have always been petite, though I did notice the weight creep caused by lower-metabolism as I entered my thirties. I thought it couldn't hurt to try.

For those of you not familiar with it, the Virgin Diet was started by JJ Virgin, a certified nutrition specialist and certified healing foods specialist. The Virgin Diet eliminates the main food intolerances that people have: soy, gluten, dairy, eggs, and peanuts, and then also cuts out sugar and corn. Sugar because it does crazy things to our bodies (hint: fat doesn't make us fat, sugar does!), and corn because 90% of the corn produced today is genetically modified. Although, more and more companies are using non-GMO corn sources. I am a big fan of nachos, so I still buy the occasional bag of tortilla chips if I see they're made with non-GMO corn!

The elimination diet during Phase One was a revelation. It was then that I realized wheat and gluten was the culprit for my constant bloating and constipation. Dairy and soy also contributed to these. It was amazing. Thirty-four years of digestive issues were cleared up! I am now a joy to travel with. I'm not hungry all the time and when I am, I don't get lightheaded and crazy. I no longer have insomnia. Fabulous.

How This Cookbook is Different

As much as I appreciate JJ Virgin for opening my eyes to my food intolerances, I don't always follow her diet plan to the letter. She advises against most sweeteners with calories, but I like to use honey from time to time. Raw, unprocessed honey contains live enzymes, vitamins, minerals, and antioxidants. I am particularly a big fan of Y. S. Organic Bee Farms in Illinois. They sell glass jars of unpasteurized, unfiltered honey in its fresh, raw state. This isn't your overly-sweet golden liquid honey—this is thick, solid honey that required a spoon to get out of the jar. It's mild, unlike any other honey I've tasted before, and doesn't overpower food or drink. JJ has made me aware, however, of how careful we must be of food labeling. I was shocked to discover the "raw" agave I'd been using was anything but (it's boiled and highly processed), and it contains more fructose than high fructose corn syrup!

If I want a calorie-free sweetener option I use Wholesome Sweeteners Zero, which is made from erythritol, a naturally occurring sugar alcohol derived from corn (so not for those who are staunchly anti-corn). Erythritol isn't as sweet as sugar, however, so I often combine it with xylitol, a naturally occurring sugar alcohol found in birch tree bark. JJ lauded xylitol in her first book, but uses mostly monk fruit in her cookbook, which is another great sweetener option.

It used to be that the only place one could find specialty sweeteners and gluten-free flours was Whole Foods. Thanks to the internet, it is now easy to buy these specialty items online for much less than in a gourmet grocery store. Previously obscure items like chia seeds and hemp hearts can now be delivered to your door in two days. Some of the best websites for finding these items are:

- Amazon.com (naturally)
- iHerb.com
- Vitacost.com

Another thing I differ with the Virgin plan is the use of protein powders. Not that I don't ever use them. I am a runner and drink half a protein shake before and after a long run. I just don't like using powders as a food supplement or regular ingredient in my cooking. I like Vega One Nutritional Shake because it also has Omega-3s and a slew of other healthy things (it was designed by a vegan athlete), and Plant Fusion because it comes in many yummy flavors like cookies n' crème. And, of course, JJ has her own line of protein powders which provide 22 grams a protein while being low in sugar, calories, and fat. My personal favorite flavor in her shakes is chai.

If you want to entirely avoid protein powders, there are recourses out there for you other than the same old beans, quinoa, nut butters, and lentils! Some surprising sources of vegan protein are:

- Peas—one cup of boiled peas has 9 grams of protein.
- French beans—one cup of cooked French beans has 13 grams of protein.
- Spinach—one cup of cooked spinach has 7 grams of protein.

- Kale—a pound of kale has 15 grams of protein. A pound isn't as much as it seems. It cooks down a great deal when steaming, stir frying, or baking into kale chips. I love kale chips and easily can eat 15 grams of protein worth in a single sitting!
- Oats—one half-cup serving of oats has 7 grams of protein.
- Hemp hearts—one-fourth cup serving of hemp hearts has 13 grams of protein. Mix that into your morning oatmeal and you're getting nearly half the protein you need for the day!

Finally, a comment about any cookbook that isn't a vegetarian cookbook: *meat-eaters don't know how to cook really delicious vegetarian food!* It makes sense, though, right? I mean, I wouldn't know the first thing to do about cooking a delicious steak. Meat eaters tend to rely on the flavor of the meat to carry a dish. So when it comes to cooking something without meat, the flavor often falls flat. Many vegetarian recipes included in non-vegetarian cookbooks are ridiculously sparse in their use of seasonings. One-quarter teaspoon of cumin? One-eighth teaspoon of salt? That might work on a steak, but not in an entire pot of lentil stew!

I've been tweaking vegetarian recipes for seventeen years, so I've gotten pretty good at it. My partner is not a vegetarian, but he has never once complained about the lack of meat in the apartment. This is thanks to my flavorful cooking. He even often opts for vegetarian options in restaurants because he, too, has come to realize that truly good vegetarian cooking is often more flavorful than meat-based recipes.

This is what inspired me to write this cookbook. I tried to find a cookbook that fit my diet, but it doesn't seem to be out there. Most gluten-free vegetarian or vegan cookbooks rely heavily on soy, and non-vegetarian gluten-free cookbooks rely heavily on meat. I realized there were probably other people like me out there yearning for a book like this. I hope you enjoy it!

2
BREAKFAST

Breakfast is the most important meal of the day—study after study shows that people who skip breakfast tend to weigh *more* than those who don't! The Virgin Diet is big on breakfast shakes, but I love baking hearty muffins and scones. A big batch can last two weeks in my apartment. I'm not entirely anti-shake. They have their moments, especially if I'm on the go and need to throw something in my bag that won't crumble into little bits and pieces.

Feel free to play with these recipes. Just because I put coconut milk in the recipe doesn't mean you can't use almond or oat or hemp (or even dairy milk, if that's your thing). Rather than give you five different oatmeal recipes or five different muffin recipes, I'm giving you one of each and trusting that you're smart enough to change the add-ins to suit your own tastes. Try cashew butter instead of almond. Nut allergy? Then sun butter is the way to go. Can't find chia seeds? Use flax or hemp. I taught myself to cook by taking notes, trying variations, and seeing what worked for me. Don't be afraid to experiment!

BAKED NUT BUTTER OATMEAL

Oatmeal is my go-to breakfast food. It's packed with protein and fiber, keeps me fueled for hours, and the variations are endless. For a different take on oatmeal, try baking it. I like to make a batch of this on Sunday night so I have it for the week. It can be topped with nuts, fruit, honey—whatever strikes your fancy.

2 cups old-fashioned gluten-free oats (I like Bob's Red Mill)
1 tsp cinnamon
1 tsp cardamom
2 cups coconut milk (or other dairy-free milk)
1 cup water
¼ cup almond butter (or other nut butter)
1 Tb chia seeds
¼ cup hemp hearts
1 Tb ground flaxseeds

1. Preheat oven to 350°F.
2. Grease a 8"x8" glass baking dish.
3. Put the almond butter and water in a medium-sized microwaveable bowl and microwave until the almond butter is soft and mixed easily with the water—about one minute.
4. Add all of the remaining ingredients into the almond butter water mixture.
5. Pour into the prepared baking dish.
6. Bake for 20 minutes, or until the center is almost firm.

Serves 4

Calories: 415   **Protein:** 15 grams   **Sugar:** 5 grams
Fat: 21 grams   **Saturated Fat:** 4 grams   **Fiber:** 9 grams
Sodium: 18 mg   **Carbs:** 42 grams

OVERNIGHT OATS

A nice treat when you're craving something smooth and chocolaty. It's delicious topped with a couple of sliced fresh strawberries and can double as a protein-packed dessert.

2 cups old-fashioned gluten-free oats
2 cups unsweetened almond milk
2 scoops chocolate protein powder (I like Plant Fusion)
¼ cup dairy free chocolate chips (I like Enjoy Life)
¼ cup unsweetened shredded coconut

1. Combine all of the ingredients in a large bowl or jar with a lid.
2. Soak in the fridge overnight.
3. Top with fresh fruit if desired.

Serves 4

Calories: 350   **Protein:** 19 grams   **Sugar:** 9 grams
Fat: 12 grams   **Saturated Fat:** 5 grams   **Fiber:** 7 grams
Sodium: 258 mg   **Carbs:** 42 grams

FRUIT OAT CRUNCH

A nice light breakfast. Feel free to experiment with different fruits for this dish. Remember that berries are on the Dirty Dozen list, so make sure to buy them organic.

1 cup old-fashioned gluten-free oats
¼ cup hemp hearts
¼ cup slivered almonds
1 small honeydew melon, chopped into 1" cubes
4 small apricots, pitted and quartered
16 oz strawberries, stemmed and halved
2 cups coconut milk

1. Mix the oats, hemp hearts, almonds, and coconut milk.
2. Divide the fruit into four dishes.
3. Top the fruit with the oat mixture.

Serves 4

Calories: 385   **Protein:** 11 grams   **Sugar:** 33 grams
Fat: 13 grams   **Saturated Fat:** 4 grams   **Fiber:** 9 grams
Sodium: 62 mg   **Carbs:** 57 grams

BLUEBERRY WALNUT QUINOA

Quinoa is a nice alternative to oatmeal when you're looking to try something different. Like oatmeal, the mix-ins and toppings are plentiful—any fruit or nuts you like are fair game.

2 cups water
1 cup quinoa, rinsed
½ cup chopped walnuts
1 cup fresh or frozen blueberries
¼ cup raw honey (or other non-sugar sweetener of your choice)

1. Boil the water and add the quinoa. Cover and simmer until the water is almost completely absorbed and the quinoa is tender—about 15 minutes.
2. Stir in the remaining ingredients.
3. Serve with coconut milk if desired.

Serves 4

Calories: 335
Fat: 12 grams
Sodium: 3 mg

Protein: 9 grams
Saturated Fat: 1 gram
Carbs: 51 grams

Sugar: 23 grams
Fiber: 5 grams

VEGGIE HASH WITH BLACK BEANS

For when you're in the mood for something a bit more savory. I don't ever peel my vegetables—most of the vitamins are located in the skin. Just give them a good wash first. For added protein, vegetarians who are egg and dairy tolerant can serve an egg or shredded cheddar over this.

1 cup dried black beans, soaked overnight
2 medium sweet potatoes, chopped into ½" cubes
1 onion, diced
2 garlic cloves, diced
1 red bell pepper, chopped
1 zucchini, grated
2 medium tomatoes, diced
2 Tb palm fruit oil
1 tsp sea salt
cracked black pepper
5 oz arugula

1. Simmer the black beans in freshly boiled water. Be sure to cover the pot to save energy and speed the cooking process.
2. Heat the oil in a large pan.
3. Add the sweet potatoes, onion, and garlic. Sauté for ten minutes before adding the bell pepper.
4. When the sweet potatoes are almost tender—about another five minutes—add the zucchini. Cook for another five minutes.
5. Turn off the heat and add the salt, pepper, and diced tomatoes.
6. Drain the black beans (checking first to make certain they're tender) and add to the sauté mixture.
7. Divide the arugula between six plates and top with the hash.

Serves 6

Calories: 215   **Protein:** 9 grams   **Sugar:** 5 grams
Fat: 5 grams   **Saturated Fat:** 2 grams   **Fiber:** 8 grams
Sodium: 426 mg   **Carbs:** 34 grams

CRANBERRY POWER SCONES

Don't be intimidated by the long list of ingredients—these aren't difficult or terribly time consuming to make. Good gluten-free vegan baking requires lots of mixing of flours since no one flour can make up for the magic of gluten and egg. The potato starch, tapioca starch, and xanthan gum are essential for mimicking the binding action of wheat flour and eggs.

I like the tartness of cranberries in these scones, but you can easily use blueberries if you want something sweeter. Teff flour is a nutritional power house—packed with iron, fiber, and protein. You can make your own oat flour by putting oats in a food processor. You can substitute raw honey for the sweeteners if you like.

A note on cooking sprays: most sprays contained damaged oils. It's best to rub oil on the baking pan or use a refillable oil mister. I sometimes buy Spectrum cooking sprays because they use organic non hydrogenated oils.

1 cup teff flour
1 cup oat flour
1 cup Bob's Red Mill All-Purpose Gluten-Free Flour
¼ cup chia seeds
¼ cup hemp hearts
¼ cup ground flax seeds
¼ cup potato starch
¼ cup tapioca starch
2 tsp xanthan gum
1 tsp cinnamon
2 tsp ground ginger
1 tsp baking powder
½ tsp baking soda
1 tsp sea salt
½ cup coconut oil, melted
½ cup palm oil
½ cup xylitol
½ cup Wholesome Sweeteners Zero
2 tsp vanilla extract

1 ½ cup unsweetened coconut milk
1 ½ cup cranberries

1. Preheat the oven to 350°F.
2. If using a scone pan coat it with cooking spray or rub it with oil. These can also be put in a muffin tin, but they're dense, not light and fluffy!
3. Mix together all of the dry ingredients in a large bowl.
4. In a separate bowl combine the wet ingredients.
5. Slowly pour the wet ingredients into the dry, stirring the entire time (a mixer can be used). The batter will be quite thick.
6. Add the fruit, stirring briefly to incorporate.
7. Divide the mixture into the prepared pan.
8. Bake for 30 minutes.

Makes 16
Per scone:

Calories: 290	**Protein:** 5 grams	**Sugar:** 1 gram
Fat: 17 grams	**Saturated Fat:** 10 grams	**Fiber:** 4 grams
Sodium: 262 mg	**Carbs:** 29 grams	

COCONUT MILLET UPMA

Upma is a traditional Indian breakfast made with semolina. I use millet to make it gluten-free and use coconut milk instead of water to make it a bit sweeter for the American breakfast palate.

1 cup millet
½ cup cashews, chopped
1 small onion, finely diced
1 jalapeño, seeded and diced
1 tomato, chopped
2 Tb coconut oil
1 tsp dried ginger
1 Tb curry powder
1 tsp turmeric powder
1 can light coconut milk
½ tsp sea salt
¼ cup unsweetened shredded coconut
1 Tb lime juice

1. Toast the millet and cashews in a dry pan for a few minutes. Do not allow them to brown. Set them aside.
2. Heat the oil in a large pan and add the onion, jalapeños, ginger, curry powder, and turmeric. Fry for a few minutes until the onion is soft. Add the tomato and cook until soft.
3. Add the coconut milk, ½ cup water, and salt and bring to a boil.
4. Slowly add the toasted millet and cashews, stirring constantly.
5. Cover the pan and allow the mixture to simmer, stirring occasionally, for twenty-five minutes.
6. Turn off the heat and let it sit for another ten minutes.
7. Stir in the shredded coconut and lime juice.

Serves 4

Calories: 445	**Protein:** 10 grams	**Sugar:** 8 grams
Fat: 23 grams	**Saturated Fat:** 10 grams	**Fiber:** 7 grams
Sodium: 306 mg	**Carbs:** 51 grams	

BREAKFAST BARS

Dried fruit is generally frowned upon in the Virgin Diet—you take away all the filling water of fruit and concentrate the sugars. However, the little bit in this recipe won't hurt you if you eat one of these bars every now and then, and they make the bars naturally sweet. These make a great quick breakfast when you're in a rush. They're also great for traveling or taking on hikes—just wrap them in wax paper and put them in baggies.

½ cup raw honey
¼ cup coconut butter (I like Earth Balance)
½ cup cashew butter
½ cup slivered almonds
½ cup chopped pecans
½ cup pitted prunes, finely chopped
½ cup pitted dates, finely chopped
½ cup unsweetened shredded coconut
1 cup old-fashioned oats
1 scoop vanilla protein powder
¼ cup hemp hearts
1 tsp vanilla extract

1. Preheat the oven to 350°F.
2. Grease an 8"x8" glass baking dish.
3. Heat the honey, coconut butter, and cashew butter in a saucepan until well combined.
4. Turn the heat off and add the remaining ingredients.
5. Pour into the prepared dish and bake for 20 minutes.
6. Cool completely and store in the refrigerator.
7. Cut into bars after completely chilled.

Makes 8
Per bar:

Calories: 460	**Protein:** 12 grams	**Sugar:** 28 grams
Fat: 27 grams	**Saturated Fat:** 6 grams	**Fiber:** 6 grams
Sodium: 88 mg	**Carbs:** 46 grams	

APPLE COCONUT PANCAKES

Top these with a bit of pure maple syrup, a drizzle of raw honey, or, as I like them, with just a bit of coconut butter. Be sure to cook these thoroughly or the insides will be gooey. For thinner pancakes add more water.

1 cup oat flour
½ cup teff flour
½ cup coconut flour
¼ cup potato starch
¼ cup tapioca starch
¼ cup xylitol
2 tsp baking powder
1 tsp baking soda
½ tsp sea salt
¼ cup coconut oil, melted, plus more for the cooking pan
1 ½ cup unsweetened coconut milk
1 Tb apple cider vinegar
1 cup water
2 apples, thinly sliced

1. Mix the dry ingredients in a large bowl.
2. Combine the wet ingredients.
3. Slowly add the wet ingredients into the dry, mixing until there are no lumps. If it seems too thick add a little more water.
4. Melt some coconut oil on a griddle or large pan.
5. Pour ¼ cup of batter at a time. Place three or four apple slices on top of the pancakes.
6. Cook until the top starts to bubble, then flip and continue cooking, about three to five minutes on each side.

Makes 14 pancakes
Per pancake:

Calories: 140   **Protein:** 2 grams   **Sugar:** 3 grams
Fat: 6 grams   **Saturated Fat:** 4 grams   **Fiber:** 3 grams
Sodium: 251 mg   **Carbs:** 22 grams

MORNING MUFFINS

½ cup Bob's Red Mill All Purpose Flour
½ cup almond meal flour
½ cup quinoa flour
¼ cup potato starch
¼ cup tapioca starch
½ cup hemp hearts
1 tsp xanthan gum
2 tsp baking soda
1 tsp baking powder
1 tsp cinnamon
1 tsp ground ginger
½ tsp sea salt
¼ cup xylitol
¼ cup Wholesome Sweeteners Zero
½ cup coconut oil, melted
1 Tb vanilla extract
½ cup unsweetened applesauce
¾ cup hemp milk
1 medium zucchini, grated
1 cup chopped walnuts

1. Preheat the oven to 350°F. Line a muffin pan with cups.
2. Mix all of the dry ingredients in a large bowl.
3. Mix the wet ingredients in a separate bowl. Slowly add the wet ingredients to the dry, stirring constantly.
4. Fold in the zucchini and walnuts. If the mixture is too thick add a little more hemp milk.
5. Pour into the prepared baking cups and bake for 30 minutes, or until the tops are very brown and a toothpick inserted in the middle comes out clean.

Makes 12
Per muffin:

Calories: 265   **Protein:** 5 grams   **Sugar:** 2 grams
Fat: 19 grams   **Saturated Fat:** 9 grams   **Fiber:** 3 grams
Sodium: 297 mg   **Carbs:** 19 grams

3
SOUPS

Soups and stews make up a large portion of my diet. It's so easy to make a big pot on the weekend and have it for lunch throughout the week. I generally make two or three different types of soup at a time in order to have a variety available. Some people like to make very large batches and freeze some to have down the line.

My go-to soup base is Better than Bouillon, a concentrated soup stock base. It comes in organic and low-sodium varieties and doesn't have the hydrogenated oils found in bouillon cubes. If you can't find Better than Bouillon, you can use organic bouillon cubes or substitute half the water for vegetable broth.

I get annoyed when cookbooks have the same recipes that all other cookbooks do, so I'm not going to give you any recipes for minestrone or lentil stew or black bean soup or chili. The point of buying a cookbook is to find new ideas—not just rehashed old ones! I hope some of these soups are innovations for your regular soup routine.

ARTICHOKE MUSHROOM SOUP

For a really fabulous version of this soup use fresh artichokes. They are, however, an absolute pain to prepare, so I won't blame you if you prefer to use canned ones.

5 artichokes or 1 can artichoke bottoms
1 Tb vegetable stock base (I like Better than Bouillon)
8 oz cremini mushrooms, chopped
4 Tb soy-free vegan margarine (I like Earth Balance or Melt)
2 garlic cloves, crushed
½ cup brown rice flour
1 Tb lemon juice
cracked black pepper

1. If using fresh artichokes they must be boiled for half an hour until tender. Let them cool, then pull the leaves off, scraping the ends for the soup. Scoop out the choke and discard. Chop up the tender bottoms and save the artichoke cooking water as the base for this soup.
2. Melt the margarine in a large soup pot or Dutch oven.
3. Sauté the mushrooms and garlic until just starting to brown. If using canned artichoke bottoms, drain and chop them and sauté them as well.
4. Add the flour and cook for a minute before adding eight cups of either water or artichoke cooking water along with the vegetable stock and pepper. If using fresh artichokes add them now.
5. Simmer, uncovered, for 20 minutes.
6. Remove from heat and add the lemon juice.

Serves 6

Calories: 180
Fat: 8 grams
Sodium: 417 mg

Protein: 6 grams
Saturated Fat: 2 grams
Carbs: 25 grams

Sugar: 2 grams
Fiber: 7 grams

ONION SOUP

This takes a long time to prepare, but it's worth it. The long simmering time is essential to the good flavor of this soup. For a non-vegan version, replace the nutritional yeast flakes with 4 ounces of shredded Swiss cheese.

6 medium onions, cut in half and sliced
1 Tb vegetable stock base
4 Tb soy-free vegan margarine
1 tsp crushed dried thyme
1 glove garlic, crushed
1 tsp sea salt
½ tsp Stevia or xylitol
½ cup brown rice flour
½ cup dry white wine
2 Tb brandy
2 Tb nutritional yeast flakes
cracked black pepper

1. Put the onions and margarine in a large soup pot or Dutch oven. Cover and simmer for 20 minutes.
2. Uncover and add the thyme, salt, and sweetener. Raise the heat to medium-low and cook onions for another 45 minutes, or until they are a rich, medium-brown color, stirring occasionally.
3. Add the garlic and flour and cook for another minute.
4. Add 6 cups of water, the vegetable stock, and the wine. Simmer uncovered for another 20 minutes.
5. Remove from heat and add the brandy, nutritional yeast flakes, and pepper.

Serves 6

Calories: 215   **Protein:** 5 grams   **Sugar:** 6 grams
Fat: 8 grams   **Saturated Fat:** 2 grams   **Fiber:** 4 grams
Sodium: 716 mg   **Carbs:** 24 grams

OKRA GUMBO

Use tender baby okra for this recipe—anything longer than 3 inches can get tough and stringy. Frozen cut okra is fine for this recipe if you want to cut down on prep time.

1 lb baby okra, sliced
1 Tb vegetable stock base
2 Tb palm oil
2 medium onions, chopped
1 large or 2 small jalapeño peppers, seeded and diced
6 gloves garlic, crushed
1 green bell pepper, seeded and chopped
One 28 oz can diced organic tomatoes
½ cup dried brown rice
1 tsp sea salt

1. Heat the oil in a large soup pot or Dutch oven and add the onions. Cook until soft, about 5 minutes.
2. Add the jalapeños, garlic, bell pepper, and canned tomatoes. Cook for another ten minutes.
3. Add 8 cups of water and vegetable stock.
4. Bring to a boil and add the brown rice.
5. Cover and simmer for 30 minutes, then add the okra and salt.
6. Cook, uncovered, for another 15 minutes, or until the rice is done and the okra is tender.

Serves 8

Calories: 145   **Protein:** 4 grams   **Sugar:** 5 grams
Fat: 4 grams   **Saturated Fat:** 2 grams   **Fiber:** 6 grams
Sodium: 505 mg   **Carbs:** 24 grams

GRAN'S POTATO SOUP

When I studied in Glasgow my flat mates were always asking me to make my "gran's potato soup." Her original version uses milk, cream, and russet potatoes; this is a slightly healthier but no less delicious version. It's also incredibly easy to make.

4 large sweet potatoes, cut into small cubes
4 large celery stalks plus leaves, chopped
4 large carrots, chopped
1 medium onion, chopped
2 garlic cloves, minced
1 Tb vegetable stock base
cracked black pepper

1. Heat six cups of water in a large soup pot or Dutch oven add the soup base.
2. Add all of the remaining ingredients except the salt and pepper. Simmer, uncovered, for twenty minutes, or until the vegetables are tender.
3. With a potato masher mash some of the potatoes in the pot to make a creamy base. Alternately, an immersion blender can be used, but don't completely liquefy the soup, just blend it a little bit. If the soup seems thick, more water can be added.
4. Add the salt and pepper.

Serves 6

Calories: 120   **Protein:** 3 grams   **Sugar:** 7 grams
Fat: 0 grams   **Saturated Fat:** 0 grams   **Fiber:** 5 grams
Sodium: 369 mg   **Carbs:** 27 grams

QUINOA BOK CHOY SOUP

This is a nice, hearty soup, great for chilly days.

1 large onion, chopped
1 Tb palm oil
6 carrots, chopped
3 large celery stalks with leaves, chopped
½ half bunch bok choy, chopped
2 garlic cloves, minced
1 Tb vegetable stock base
1 tsp sea salt
1 cup quinoa, uncooked
2 sweet potatoes, chopped
½ cup fresh cilantro, chopped
cracked black pepper

1. Heat the oil in a large soup pot or Dutch oven. Sauté the onion and garlic until just beginning to brown.
2. Add the carrots, celery, and bok choy. Sauté until carrots are just starting to brown.
3. Add 8 cups of water, vegetable stock base, salt, and quinoa.
4. Bring to a boil, then add the sweet potatoes, lower heat, cover, and simmer for 20 minutes until the potatoes are tender.
5. Turn off the heat and add the cilantro and pepper. If the soup seems thick, up to two more cups of water can be added.

Serves 8

Calories: 165	**Protein:** 5 grams	**Sugar:** 5 grams
Fat: 3 grams	**Saturated Fat:** 1 gram	**Fiber:** 5 grams
Sodium: 567 mg	**Carbs:** 30 grams	

MULLIGATAWNY SOUP

An incredibly easy high-protein Indian soup. Some people like to blend the soup at the end, but I find the red lentils are so soft after an hour that it's not necessary.

2 cups dried red lentils
¼ tsp ground cloves
1 bay leaf
1 Tb turmeric
2 garlic cloves, crushed
1 tsp ground cumin
1 small jalapeño pepper, seeded and minced
1 tsp vegetable stock base
1 tsp sea salt
cracked black pepper
2 Tb lemon juice
1 can coconut milk (not light)

1. Put the first eight ingredients in a large soup pot or Dutch oven along with 8 cups of water.
2. Cover and simmer for one hour.
3. Remove from heat and add the remaining ingredients. Add more water and salt if needed.

Serves 8

Calories: 265　　**Protein:** 13 grams　　**Sugar:** 1 gram
Fat: 10 grams　　**Saturated Fat:** 8 grams　　**Fiber:** 6 grams
Sodium: 373 mg　　**Carbs:** 32 grams

SEAWEED SOUP

Don't let the name deter you—this soup is very yummy! Also, seaweed is an excellent source of iodine, folate, calcium, iron, and vitamins A, C, E, and K. Pescetarians might consider adding half a pound of shrimp to this recipe, but it's good without shrimp, too.

½ oz dried wakame
8 oz mixed mushrooms (oyster, shiitake, cremini), chopped
2 Tb coconut aminos
½ tsp sea salt
1 Tb sriracha sauce
4 scallions, chopped
cracked black pepper

1. Soak the wakame in hot water for ten minutes then drain.
2. Bring six cups water to a boil. Add the wakame, mushrooms, sea salt, and coconut aminos.
3. Simmer for ten minutes before turning off the heat and adding the sriracha, pepper, and scallions.

Serves 6

Calories: 25   **Protein:** 1 gram   **Sugar:** 1 gram
Fat: 1 gram   **Saturated Fat:** 0 grams   **Fiber:** 1 gram
Sodium: 511 mg   **Carbs:** 5 grams

"CREAM" OF ASPARAGUS SOUP

Pureed raw cashews make an excellent substitution for dairy in creamy soups.

1 Tb palm oil
1 large onion, chopped
8 oz cremini mushrooms, sliced
1 lb asparagus, woody ends removed and cut into 1" pieces
1 Tb vegetable stock base
1 tsp cumin
1 tsp turmeric
1 cup raw cashews, soaked overnight
cracked black pepper
2 Tb lemon juice

1. Heat the oil in a large soup pot or Dutch oven and sauté the onions, mushrooms, and asparagus for five minutes.
2. Add four cups water, vegetable stock base, cumin, and turmeric. Cover and simmer for 20 minutes.
3. Meanwhile, drain and rinse the cashews. Place them in a blender with the lemon juice and one cup water and blend until smooth.
4. Turn the heat off the soup pot and with an immersion blender puree the soup until not completely smooth—there should still be some chunks of vegetables. If you don't have an immersion blender you can puree half of the soup in a blender and return it to the soup pot.
5. Add the cashew mixture to the soup pot and add black pepper to taste.

Serves 4

Calories: 285　　**Protein:** 12 grams　　**Sugar:** 8 grams
Fat: 18 grams　　**Saturated Fat:** 4 grams　　**Fiber:** 5 grams
Sodium: 389 mg　　**Carbs:** 25 grams

ROASTED RED PEPPER SOUP

Vegetarians can replace the cashew cream with goat cheese. Goat products are gentler on the stomach and often even individuals who are dairy intolerant can eat them without issues.

1 Tb palm oil
1 medium onion, chopped
1 Tb vegetable stock base
1 12oz jar roasted red peppers, drained and chopped
4 beets, peeled and diced
1 Tb ground coriander
1 tsp dried thyme
½ cup raw cashews, soaked overnight, drained and rinsed
cracked black pepper
2 Tb lemon juice

1. Heat the oil in a large soup pot or Dutch oven and sauté the onions for five minutes.
2. Add six cups water, vegetable stock base, red peppers, beets, thyme, and coriander. Simmer, uncovered, for 20 minutes.
3. Meanwhile, combine the cashews, lemon juice, and half a cup of water in a blender until smooth.
4. Add the cashew mixture to the soup pot and add black pepper to taste.
5. Use an immersion blender to blend part of the soup—don't completely blend, there should still be chunks in the soup. Alternately, blend half of the soup in a blender and return to the pot.

Serves 4

Calories: 210   **Protein:** 6 grams   **Sugar:** 11 grams
Fat: 11 grams   **Saturated Fat:** 3 grams   **Fiber:** 6 grams
Sodium: 448 mg   **Carbs:** 23 grams

BASIL EGGPLANT SOUP

You can vary the amount of basil depending on your personal preference.

2 medium eggplants, about one pound each, cut into 1" cubes
1 large onion, chopped
2 garlic cloves, crushed
1 tsp dried oregano
2 Tb olive oil, divided
6 plum tomatoes, chopped
1 Tb vegetable stock base
½ tsp sea salt
cracked black pepper
⅛ tsp cayenne pepper
1 bunch basil, one to two ounces

1. Prepare the eggplant by lightly salting it and placing it in a colander. Let it set for at least twenty minutes, then rinse it thoroughly.
2. Heat one tablespoon of the oil in a large soup pot or Dutch oven and sauté the onion, garlic, and oregano for five minutes.
3. Add six cups water, vegetable stock base, eggplant, tomatoes, salt, pepper, and cayenne. Simmer, partially covered, for 30 minutes.
4. Purée the basil and remaining tablespoon of olive oil in a food processor.
5. Remove the soup from the heat and stir in the basil oil paste.

Serves 6

Calories: 120
Fat: 5 grams
Sodium: 453 mg

Protein: 4 grams
Saturated Fat: 1 gram
Carbs: 17 grams

Sugar: 9 grams
Fiber: 7 grams

SPRING PEA SOUP

This is especially good with fresh peas, but frozen are fine, too.

1 Tb palm oil
2 small onions, chopped
3 garlic cloves, minced
½ tsp fresh ginger
½ tsp sea salt
¼ tsp red pepper flakes
1 tsp ground coriander
½ tsp ground cumin
2 small tomatoes, diced
2 tsp vegetable stock base
20 oz fresh or frozen baby peas

1. Heat the oil in a large soup pot or Dutch oven and sauté the onion and garlic until starting to brown. Add the ginger, salt, pepper, coriander, and cumin and cook for another minute before adding the tomatoes and stirring well to combine.
2. Add six cups of water along with the vegetable stock base. Bring to a boil and simmer, uncovered, for ten minutes.
3. Add the peas and simmer, uncovered, for another ten minutes.
4. Use an immersion blender to purée most of the soup. Alternately, wait for the soup to cool some, then purée in batches in a blender, leaving one cup unblended.

Serves 6

Calories: 125   **Protein:** 6 grams   **Sugar:** 7 grams
Fat: 3 grams   **Saturated Fat:** 1 gram **Fiber:** 6 grams
Sodium: 468 mg   **Carbs:** 19 grams

COCONUT SPINACH SOUP

I prefer fresh spinach for this recipe, but frozen is fine in a pinch. The lemongrass will remain woody and inedible, so don't chop it too small. You want to be able to easily pick it out of your bowl!

1 Tb coconut oil
2 onions, chopped
2 garlic cloves, minced
2 jalapeño peppers, seeded and diced
1 stalk lemongrass, cut into 1" pieces
1 lb fresh or frozen spinach, thawed if frozen
1 can light coconut milk
1 Tb vegetable stock base
¼ tsp sea salt
fresh cracked pepper

1. Heat the oil in a large soup pot or Dutch oven and sauté the onion and garlic until starting to brown.
2. Add the jalapeños and lemongrass and cook for a few minutes before adding the spinach. If using frozen spinach squeeze the liquid from it first. If using fresh spinach, stir until the spinach is wilted.
3. Add four cups of water along with the vegetable stock base, coconut milk, salt and pepper.
4. Bring to a boil, cover, and simmer for fifteen minutes.

Serves 4

Calories: 145   **Protein:** 5 grams   **Sugar:** 5 grams
Fat: 8 grams   **Saturated Fat:** 3 grams   **Fiber:** 4 grams
Sodium: 613 mg   **Carbs:** 16 grams

4
SALADS

I feel the same way about most cookbook salad recipes as I do about their soup recipes—the same things appearing over and over. The vast majority of us do not need instructions on how to make a salad. Take some mixed greens, top with chopped vegetables, drizzle with dressing, and you're done! Yet so many cookbooks provide you with five different variations of garden vegetable salads and five different types of dressings that are basically the same thing.

Hopefully I won't do the same thing that I criticize other cookbooks for. I certainly won't tell you what veggies to put on your mesclun—you're an adult. I like cucumber and tomato, but if you want beet and carrot, go right ahead, you don't need a recipe from me providing you with that option.

ANYTHING-BUT-BASIC VINAIGRETTE

I said I wouldn't burden you with endless dressing recipes, and I won't, I'll just share this one. This is my basic, go-to oil and vinegar dressing that I keep on hand at all times and use whenever dressing is required. You can easily alter it to suit your purposes. Want a Dijon dressing? Double or triple the mustard content. Care for something lighter? Double the lemon juice and use white wine vinegar instead of balsamic. Want more bite? Then put in more garlic and black pepper. This stays for weeks in the refrigerator—just give it a good shake to remix. If the oil congeals run hot water over the jar before serving or set it out on the counter while prepping your salad.

½ cup extra virgin olive oil
½ cup balsamic vinegar
2 Tb lemon juice
2 Tb good quality brown mustard
1 garlic clove, very finely diced
½ tsp sea salt
cracked black pepper

1. Combine all of the ingredients in a glass jar with a lid.
2. Shake vigorously to combine.

Makes about 1 ½ cups
Per tablespoon

Calories: 45   **Protein:** 0 grams   **Sugar:** 1 gram
Fat: 5 grams   **Saturated Fat:** 1 gram   **Fiber:** 0 grams
Sodium: 81 mg   **Carbs:** 1 gram

SWEET POTATO & FRENCH BEAN SALAD

A nice picnic or potluck dish. Excellent served on top of spicy arugula. French green beans, or haricots verts, are long and thin and more tender than regular green beans.

8 oz French green beans, trimmed and halved
2 medium sweet potatoes, chopped into 1" cubes
1 shallot, diced
2 garlic cloves, diced
1 Tb fresh rosemary, chopped
¼ cup basic vinaigrette (dressing of your choice)
½ tsp sea salt

1. Cook the potatoes in boiling water until tender, about ten minutes.
2. Add the green beans to the pot two minutes before the potatoes are finished.
3. Drain the vegetables and place them in a large bowl.
4. Add the remaining ingredients.
5. Allow to cool before serving.

Serves 4

Calories: 140   **Protein:** 2 grams   **Sugar:** 5 grams
Fat: 6 grams   **Saturated Fat:** 1 gram   **Fiber:** 4 grams
Sodium: 135 mg   **Carbs:** 20 grams

ARTICHOKE SWEET POTATO SALAD

A new take on the usual potato salad. If you are egg tolerant, you can add a diced hard-boiled egg to this.

2 large sweet potatoes, chopped into 1" cubes
1 Tb red wine vinegar
1 Tb Dijon mustard
1 Tb lemon juice
1 Tb extra virgin olive oil
cracked black pepper
1 14oz can artichoke hearts or bottoms, quartered
1 shallot, diced
½ tsp dried dill

1. Cook the potatoes in boiling water until tender, about ten minutes. Drain and place them in a large bowl.
2. Add the remaining ingredients.
3. Refrigerate for at least an hour before serving.

Serves 4

Calories: 150
Fat: 4 grams
Sodium: 398 mg

Protein: 5 grams
Saturated Fat: 1 gram
Carbs: 27 grams

Sugar: 5 grams
Fiber: 6 grams

GREEN PAPAYA SALAD

Don't use a ripe papaya for this or it will be too sweet.

1 large green (unripe) papaya
1 garlic clove, crushed
1 jalapeño pepper, seeded and minced
2 Tb lime juice
2 Tb coconut aminos
1 Tb extra virgin olive oil
1 Tb rice vinegar
1 pint cherry tomatoes, halved
¼ cup slivered almonds
½ cup cilantro, chopped

1. Prepare the dressing by combining the garlic, peppers, lime juice, coconut aminos, oil, and vinegar in a blender and processing until smooth.
2. Prepare the papaya by peeling, cutting in half, and discarding the seeds. Shred using a grater.
3. Divide between four plates, top with cherry tomatoes, almonds, cilantro, and spicy dressing.

Serves 4

Calories: 135   **Protein:** 2 grams   **Sugar:** 17 grams
Fat: 4 grams   **Saturated Fat:** 1 gram   **Fiber:** 4 grams
Sodium: 523 mg   **Carbs:** 26 grams

WILD RICE SALAD

This salad eats like a meal.

1 cup wild rice
1 tsp vegetable stock base (like Better than Bouillon)
8 oz carrots, sliced
1 lb asparagus, woody ends removed and cut into 1" pieces
¼ cup white wine vinegar
1 Tb raw honey
1 tsp sea salt
½ tsp dried thyme
1 garlic clove, minced
¼ cup olive oil
1 tsp brown mustard, like a Dijon
1 Tb lemon juice
5 oz mixed baby greens
½ cup cashews

1. Put the rice in a pot with two cups water and the vegetable stock base. Cover and simmer for 50 minutes, or until the rice is tender. Let cool.
2. In a separate pot add the vinegar, honey, sea salt, thyme, garlic, and olive oil along with one cup water. Bring to a boil and add the carrots. Cook for three minutes before adding the asparagus. Simmer for another two minutes.
3. Remove the vegetables from the heat and strain the liquid into a separate bowl. Add the mustard and lemon juice to the cooking liquid.
4. Divide the greens, rice, cashews, and vegetables on four separate plates. Serve with the vegetable cooking liquid on the side.

Serves 4

Calories: 370   **Protein:** 13 grams   **Sugar:** 11 grams
Fat: 15 grams   **Saturated Fat:** 2 grams   **Fiber:** 8 grams
Sodium: 493 mg   **Carbs:** 51 grams

ROASTED BEET AND ORANGE SALAD

4 beets
1 Tb olive oil
2 oranges (use blood oranges if you can find them)
¼ cup hemp hearts
5 oz mixed baby greens
¼ cup basic vinaigrette (or dressing of your choice)

1. Preheat the oven to 400°F.
2. Prepare the beets by placing them in a small roasting pan. Drizzle the olive oil on top of the beets and roast for 45 minutes.
3. Meanwhile, divide the greens on four plates. Divide the oranges into segments and cut the segments in half. Top each plate with half of an orange and 1 Tb hemp hearts.
4. Once the beets have cooled, chop and add one beet to each salad plate.
5. Top each salad with 1 Tb vinaigrette.

Serves 4

Calories: 215 **Protein:** 6 grams **Sugar:** 13 grams
Fat: 12 grams **Saturated Fat:** 1 gram **Fiber:** 5 grams
Sodium: 209 mg **Carbs:** 21 grams

WARM THAI SALAD

1 Tb coconut oil
8 oz broccoli florets
2 large carrots, sliced
8 oz bok choy, sliced
½ red onion, sliced
2 Thai chilies, seeded and diced
1 Tb fresh ginger
2 bell peppers, preferably different colors, sliced
1 medium zucchini, halved and sliced
1 Tb coconut aminos
¼ cup basic vinaigrette (or dressing of your choice)
½ cup raw cashews or chopped almonds
5 oz mixed baby greens

1. Heat the oil in a large, heavy pan. Add the broccoli, carrots, onion, chilies, and ginger. Stir-fry for three minutes.
2. Add the bell peppers, zucchini, and bok choy. Stir-fry for another two minutes.
3. Add the coconut aminos and cook for one more minute before removing from heat.
4. Divide the greens, cashews, and vegetables on four separate plates. Serve with the basic vinaigrette.

Serves 4

Calories: 255   **Protein:** 8 grams   **Sugar:** 10 grams
Fat: 16 grams   **Saturated Fat:** 5 grams   **Fiber:** 6 grams
Sodium: 276 mg   **Carbs:** 24 grams

STRAWBERRY AVOCADO SALAD

A perfect summer salad. Feel free to try different summer fruits in this like watermelon or blackberries. In the winter, pear is a nice option.

2 Tb extra virgin olive oil
2 Tb raspberry vinegar
½ tsp sriracha
½ tsp sea salt
cracked black pepper
¼ tsp cinnamon
16 oz strawberries, quartered
½ red onion, sliced
1 avocado, chopped
6 oz fresh raspberries or blueberries
¼ cup walnuts or pecans, chopped and toasted
5 oz mixed baby greens

1. Make the raspberry vinaigrette by combining the first six ingredients. Set aside.
2. Divide the lettuce between four plates. Top with the fruits, onion, avocado, and nuts.
3. Drizzle with the raspberry vinaigrette.

Serves 4

Calories: 240　　**Protein:** 4 grams　　**Sugar:** 10 grams
Fat: 17 grams　　**Saturated Fat:** 2 grams　　**Fiber:** 9 grams
Sodium: 359 mg　　**Carbs:** 23 grams

ANTIPASTO PLATTER

1 large eggplant, sliced into ½" rounds
1 large zucchini, sliced into ¼" rounds
2 large red bell peppers
8 whole garlic cloves, peeled
2 large Portobello mushroom caps, cut into ½" slices
¼ cup olive oil
½ tsp sea salt
cracked black pepper

1. Preheat the broiler.
2. Soak the eggplant in a bowl of salted water for at least twenty minutes.
3. Roast the red peppers by putting them in a foil-lined metal baking dish and cooking them under the broiler, turning occasionally. Roast until the outside skin is completely black. Allow to cool until they can be handled, then dip them into cold water and remove the black peel. Cut the peppers into ½" strips.
4. Lower the oven temperature to 350°F. Line a large shallow baking pan with foil and coat with cooking spray or brush with oil.
5. Drain the eggplant and place on the tray along with the red peppers, zucchini, mushrooms, and garlic cloves. Brush the vegetables with oil and sprinkle with salt and pepper.
6. Bake until starting to brown, about one hour.
7. Serve at room temperature.

Serves 4

Calories: 155   **Protein:** 4 grams   **Sugar:** 11 grams
Fat: 8 grams   **Saturated Fat:** 1 gram   **Fiber:** 7 grams
Sodium: 310 mg   **Carbs:** 20 grams

WARM MUSHROOM SALAD

2 Tb extra virgin olive oil
4 Portobello mushroom caps
½ tsp sea salt
fresh cracked pepper
2 garlic cloves, crushed
2 large tomatoes, chopped
2 Tb balsamic vinegar
5 oz mixed baby greens

1. Preheat the broiler. Line a metal baking pan with foil.
2. Place the mushrooms bottoms up on the pan. Drizzle with one tablespoon of the olive oil and sprinkle with the salt and pepper.
3. Broil for five minutes. Remove and set aside.
4. In a medium bowl combine the tomatoes, garlic, olive oil, and vinegar. Place the tomato mixture on the mushroom caps.
5. Return the mushrooms to the broiler and cook for another five minutes. Remove and set aside.
6. Divide the greens between four plates. Top each plate with a mushroom cap.

Serves 4

Calories: 115
Fat: 7 grams
Sodium: 354 mg

Protein: 3 grams
Saturated Fat: 1 gram
Carbs: 11 grams

Sugar: 6 grams
Fiber: 3 grams

CREAMY MOROCCAN DRESSING

I'll leave you with one additional dressing. This is perfect for when you're craving something spicy and creamy, but know that topping your greens with buttermilk ranch is not the best choice. Coconut cream can be hard to find—some health food stores carry it and it can be purchased online. Do not buy cream of coconut, which is used for piña coladas and contains tons of sugar and preservatives.

1 tsp sea salt
2 tsp ground cumin
1 tsp ground coriander
¼ tsp ground nutmeg
½ tsp cayenne
2 Tb raw apple cider vinegar
1 Tb raw honey
1 shallot, finely diced
1 cup coconut cream

1. Combine all of the ingredients in a glass jar with a lid.
2. Shake vigorously to combine.

Makes about 1 ½ cups
Per tablespoon:

Calories: 40   **Protein:** 0 grams   **Sugar:** 1 gram
Fat: 4 grams   **Saturated Fat:** 3 grams   **Fiber:** 0 grams
Sodium: 98 mg   **Carbs:** 2 grams

5
MAIN COURSES

Finally—the main event! This is where vegetarian recipes really shine. Most gluten-free and clean-eating cookbooks throw in a few vegetarian dishes, but why spend $20 on a cookbook for just a few recipes when you can have a cookbook completely dedicated to them? It is possible to follow a clean, allergen-free diet that doesn't rely on meat!

I mentioned this in a note by my scone recipe, but let me put it here again for anyone who may have missed it as several of the main courses ask you to grease a baking pan: most sprays contained damaged oils. It's best to rub oil on the baking pan or use a refillable oil mister. I sometimes buy Spectrum cooking sprays because they use organic non hydrogenated oils, but you can use whatever you're most comfortable with.

PASTA WITH GARLIC VERMOUTH SAUCE

RP's Pasta Company makes amazing fresh gluten-free pastas, but they contain egg. If you're egg intolerant, a dried quinoa pasta like Andean Dream or Ancient Harvest (contains corn) works just fine. Use fresh vermouth—it goes bad if not refrigerated.

16 oz gluten-free pasta, cooked according to directions on package
¼ cup olive oil
6 garlic cloves, crushed
¼ cup fresh basil, chopped
¼ cup brown rice flour
⅓ cup dry vermouth
2 Tb lemon juice
2 cups hemp milk
½ tsp sea salt
1 tsp Sriracha chili garlic sauce
½ cup pine nuts, crushed and toasted
1 cup fresh or frozen peas
2 Tb nutritional yeast flakes
cracked black pepper

1. Heat the oil in a two-quart pot.
2. Sauté garlic until cooked but not brown. Add the flour and cook for another minute before adding all of the remaining ingredients except the pasta. Be sure to stir well and slowly add the hemp milk to prevent lumps. Simmer, stirring constantly for 5 minutes.
3. If the mixture is too thick, you can add water to thin it. If it seems thin, cook for a bit longer, but know that it will thicken upon standing.
4. A serving is two ounces of pasta with 1/3 cup sauce. Smaller pasta shapes like elbows can be mixed into the sauce.

Serves 8

Calories: 340
Fat: 16 grams
Sodium: 575 mg

Protein: 9 grams
Saturated Fat: 2 grams
Carbs: 42 grams

Sugar: 2 grams
Fiber: 4 grams

STUFFED BELL PEPPERS

Use green bell peppers if you're on a budget.

4 large, round red bell peppers
2 Tb olive oil
1 onion, diced
2 garlic cloves, minced
4 oz white mushrooms, finely chopped
1 jalapeño pepper, seeded and diced
1 medium zucchini, grated
1 medium tomato, diced
1 tsp ginger
2 tsp ground cumin
1 tsp ground coriander
1 cup cooked brown or wild rice
1 cup cooked brown or green lentils
1 tsp sea salt
fresh cracked pepper
¼ cup fresh cilantro, chopped

1. Preheat the oven to 350°F.
2. Cut the tops off the bell peppers and set aside. Discard the seeds and pith from the peppers.
3. Heat the oil in a large, heavy pan and sauté the onion, garlic, mushrooms, jalapeño, and zucchini until soft. Add the tomato and cook for another minute before turning off the heat. Add the remaining ingredients to the vegetable mix.
4. Divide the mixture between the peppers. Place them in a small glass baking pan and fill the pan halfway with boiling water. Put the tops back on the peppers. Cover the baking pan loosely with foil.
5. Bake for an hour, or until the peppers are tender.

Serves 4

Calories: 265
Fat: 8 grams
Sodium: 604 mg

Protein: 10 grams
Saturated Fat: 1 gram
Carbs: 39 grams

Sugar: 12 grams
Fiber: 10 grams

THAI COCONUT CURRY

This is one of my go-to recipes when I want to impress.

For the coconut rice:
1 small onion, diced
1 clove garlic, diced
1 Tb coconut oil
1 tsp turmeric
1 tsp cumin
1 tsp coriander
1 cup brown rice
1 can light coconut milk
½ tsp sea salt

1. Heat the oil in a pot.
2. Sauté garlic and onion until cooked but not brown.
3. Add the rice and cook for another minute before adding all of the remaining ingredients plus ¾ cup of water.
4. Cover the pot and simmer for 60 minutes. The rice will still be a little runny and will have a slightly chewy texture.

For the vegetable stir fry:
1 can light coconut milk
1 clove garlic, crushed
8 oz asparagus, woody ends removed, cut into 1" pieces
8 oz mushrooms, cremini or white
1 red or green bell pepper, sliced
1 8oz can sliced bamboo shoots
½ head bok choy, chopped
½ cup raw cashews or chopped almonds
1 tsp crushed red pepper flakes
1 Tb coconut aminos
2 Tb lime juice
10 fresh basil leaves, chopped

1. Heat the coconut milk in a large skillet. Add the garlic and cook, stirring, for one minute.
2. Add the vegetables and simmer for five minutes.

3. Add the remaining ingredients and cook for another five minutes before removing from heat.
4. Divide the coconut rice between four plates and top with the stir-fried vegetables.

Serves 4

Calories: 470   **Protein:** 13 grams   **Sugar:** 12 grams
Fat: 21 grams   **Saturated Fat:** 5 grams   **Fiber:** 10 grams
Sodium: 470 mg   **Carbs:** 64 grams

ENCHILADA LASAGNA

This is one of the few dishes I feel needs dairy to be truly amazing. You can try substituting Daiya shredded cheese (dairy and soy free), or leave the dairy out altogether, but I don't think it's the same. It can be difficult to find a gluten-free tortilla that doesn't have soy, egg, or corn. Food For Life and Engine 2 make great brown rice tortillas. La Tortilla Factory's wraps also fit the bill, but they tend to mush in this recipe. Toufayan, Udi's, and Rudi's also has options, but they all contain egg and/or corn. I use good quality organic jarred salsa, but if you want to make your own, that's fine as well.

4 cups cooked black beans, drained if canned
1 Tb palm oil
1 onion, chopped
2 garlic cloves, crushed
¾ cup low-fat cottage cheese
¾ cup reduced-fat sour cream
2 4oz cans chopped green chilies
½ cup cilantro, chopped
1 Tb ground cumin
1 Tb chili powder
1 16oz jar good quality organic salsa (I prefer spicy)
6 gluten-free tortillas, halved
4 oz shredded reduced-fat sharp cheddar cheese

1. Preheat the oven to 350°F.
2. Prepare a 9"x13" glass baking dish by coating with cooking spray or rubbing with oil.
3. Reserve ¼ cup of the salsa. In a large bowl, combine the cottage cheese, sour cream, chilies, cilantro, cumin, chili powder, and remaining salsa and set aside.
4. Heat the oil in a large heavy pan and sauté the onion and garlic until just starting to brown. Add the cooked black beans and cook a few minutes longer before removing from the heat.
5. Spread the reserved salsa on the bottom of the baking dish. Layer four of the tortilla halves over the salsa.

6. Put half of the black bean mixture on the tortillas, followed by 1/3 of the salsa mixture, and one ounce of the shredded cheese. Follow with four more tortilla halves, the rest of the black bean mixture, 1/3 of the salsa mixture, and one ounce of the shredded cheese.
7. Top with the last four tortilla halves, the remaining salsa mixture, and the remaining two ounces of cheese.
8. Bake for 30 minutes.

Serves 8

Calories: 360   **Protein:** 19 grams   **Sugar:** 6 grams
Fat: 11 grams   **Saturated Fat:** 5 grams   **Fiber:** 12 grams
Sodium: 731 mg   **Carbs:** 50 grams

SPICY EGGPLANT AND NOODLES

For the noodles:
8 oz gluten free pasta, something small like pagodas or shells
1 Tb sesame oil
3 scallions, chopped
2 garlic cloves, crushed
1 Tb Sriracha sauce
1 Tb coconut aminos
2 Tb rice wine vinegar
1 Tb raw honey
½ cup black tea, cooled
¼ cup tahini

1. Cook the pasta according to the directions on the box.
2. Meanwhile make the spicy sesame sauce by combining the remaining ingredients in a large bowl.
3. Add the sauce to the noodles.

For the eggplant:
1 large eggplant, cut into 1" cubes
2 Tb palm oil
3 scallions, chopped
2 garlic cloves, crushed
1 Tb Sriracha sauce

1. Heat the oil in a large frying pan and sauté the eggplant until tender, about ten minutes.
2. Add the scallions and garlic and sauté for a minute before adding the Sriracha sauce.
3. Add the pasta and heat until warm.

Serves 4

Calories: 455   **Protein:** 11 grams   **Sugar:** 10 grams
Fat: 20 grams   **Saturated Fat:** 5 grams   **Fiber:** 10 grams
Sodium: 427 mg   **Carbs:** 60 grams

EGGPLANT LASAGNA

1 Tb olive oil
2 large eggplant, thinly sliced lengthwise with a mandolin
2 large zucchini, thinly sliced lengthwise with a mandolin
2 large tomatoes, thinly sliced with a mandolin
18 large basil leaves, whole
1 28oz can crushed organic tomatoes
1 large onion, chopped
2 garlic cloves, minced
¼ cup red wine
10 oz frozen chopped spinach, thawed
1 tsp dried oregano
½ tsp sea salt
black cracked pepper
2 Tb nutritional yeast flakes

1. Preheat the oven to 350°F. Coat a 13"x9" baking dish with cooking spray or rub with oil.
2. Prepare the eggplant by coating both sides with cooking spray or rubbing with oil. Place them in a single layer on baking sheets line with foil. Bake for 20 minutes. Set aside to cool.
3. Meanwhile prepare the tomato sauce. Heat the oil in a large sauce pan. Sauté the onion and garlic until just starting to brown. Add the red wine, scraping the bottom of the pot. Stir in the crushed tomatoes and spices. Squeeze the liquid from the spinach and add to the sauce. Simmer for 20 minutes.
4. Spread ¼ cup of the tomato sauce on the bottom of the prepared baking dish. Place a layer of eggplant on the sauce, followed by zucchini going the opposite direction, tomato slices, basil leaves, and ⅓ of the tomato sauce. Repeat two more times, finishing with a layer of tomato sauce.
5. Bake for 30 minutes.

Serves 6

Calories: 195 **Protein:** 9 grams **Sugar:** 17 grams
Fat: 4 grams **Saturated Fat:** 1 gram **Fiber:** 14 grams
Sodium: 495 mg **Carbs:** 34 grams

ASPARAGUS BLACK BEAN ENCHILADAS

This works well with other vegetables too. Try sautéed mushrooms, spinach, or sweet potatoes.

2 Tb palm oil
1 Tb brown rice flour
2 Tb chili powder
1 8oz can tomato sauce, no sugar or salt added
1 tsp cumin
½ tsp garlic powder
1 16oz jar good quality organic salsa
3 cups cooked black beans, drained if canned
2 scallions, sliced
8 brown rice tortillas, like Food for Life or Engine One
1 lb asparagus, woody ends removed

1. Preheat the oven to 350°F. Prepare a 9"x13" glass baking dish by coating with cooking spray or rubbing with oil.
2. Prepare the enchilada sauce by heating the oil in a small sauce pan. Add the flour and chili powder and stir for one minute. Add the tomato sauce, garlic powder, cumin, and one cup water. Simmer gently for ten minutes, stirring occasionally.
3. Meanwhile blanch the asparagus by boiling for three minutes then draining and rinsing under cold water.
4. Spread ½ cup of the enchilada sauce on the bottom of the baking pan.
5. Make the enchiladas by placing ⅓ cup black beans, ¼ cup salsa, and 2 or 3 asparagus stalks on a tortilla. Roll and place in the baking pan, seam side down.
6. Top with the remaining enchilada sauce and scallions and bake for twenty minutes.

Makes 8
Per enchilada:

Calories: 290	**Protein:** 11 grams	**Sugar:** 4 grams
Fat: 7 grams	**Saturated Fat:** 2 grams	**Fiber:** 11 grams
Sodium: 539 mg	**Carbs:** 49 grams	

VEGETARIAN SHEPHERD'S PIE

1 cup dried brown lentils, soaked overnight
1 medium onion, chopped
2 garlic cloves, minced
4 carrots, chopped
4 celery stalks with leaves, chopped
1 Tb palm oil
1 14oz can diced organic tomatoes
1 tsp dried oregano
1 Tb chili powder
1 tsp mustard powder
2 Tb nutritional yeast flakes
4 sweet potatoes, chopped
2 Tb soy-free vegan margarine
½ cup hemp milk
1 tsp sea salt

1. Heat the oil in a large soup pot or Dutch oven. Cook the onion and garlic for a few minutes before adding the carrots and celery. Sauté until just starting to brown.
2. Add the tomatoes, drained lentils, and one cup water. Cover and simmer for 30 minutes, until the lentils are tender. Add more water if necessary.
3. Meanwhile prepare the potato topping by boiling the sweet potatoes until tender. Drain and mash with the margarine and hemp milk. Season with sea salt.
4. Preheat the oven to 400°F. Grease a casserole dish.
5. Remove the lentil mixture from the heat and add the oregano, chili powder, and nutritional yeast flakes.
6. Pour the mixture into the prepared baking pan. Cover with the mashed potatoes. Bake for 30 minutes, until lightly browned on top.

Serves 6

Calories: 305   **Protein:** 13 grams   **Sugar:** 10 grams
Fat: 7 grams   **Saturated Fat:** 2 grams   **Fiber:** 16 grams
Sodium: 570 mg   **Carbs:** 48 grams

INDIAN SHEPHERD'S PIE

1 cup frozen lima beans, thawed
1 small head cauliflower, about one pound, chopped
1 Tb soy-free vegan margarine
1 tsp sea salt, divided
cracked black pepper
2 Tb coconut oil
2 carrots, diced
4 cups cooked red lentils
1 Tb curry powder
¼ tsp cinnamon
1 tsp cumin
1 clove garlic, minced
1 tsp turmeric
1 tsp vegetable stock base
1 cup fresh or frozen peas
1 Tb tomato paste

1. Preheat the oven to 350°F. Coat a casserole dish with cooking spray or rub with oil.
2. Prepare the topping by boiling the lima beans and cauliflower until tender, about ten minutes. Drain and put in a food processor with the margarine, black pepper, and ½ teaspoon sea salt. Process until smooth. Set aside.
3. Prepare the filling by heating the oil in a large pan and cooking the carrots for five minutes. Add the spices and cook for another minute.
4. Turn off the heat and add the lentils, soup base, peas, and remaining salt.
5. Pour the lentil mixture into the prepared baking pan and top with the cauliflower mixture.
6. Bake for 30 minutes, until lightly browned on top.

Serves 6

Calories: 315   **Protein:** 18 grams   **Sugar:** 4 grams
Fat: 8 grams   **Saturated Fat:** 5 grams   **Fiber:** 10 grams
Sodium: 608 mg   **Carbs:** 46 grams

STUFFED BUTTERNUT SQUASH

2 medium butternut squash, cut in half, seeds removed
2 Tb olive oil
1 small onion, chopped
1 small tomato, chopped
4 oz mushrooms, chopped
2 cups cooked or canned black beans (drained if canned)
1 small zucchini, finely chopped
1 tsp dried oregano
2 Tb organic tomato paste
2 Tb nutritional yeast flakes
1 tsp sriracha
½ tsp sea salt, plus more for the squash
cracked black pepper

1. Preheat the oven to 400°F.
2. Place the squash halves cut side up on a large baking sheet covered in aluminum foil. Drizzle the olive oil over the squash halves. Sprinkle with sea salt and black pepper. Bake for 40 to 50 minutes, or until tender.
3. Remove from oven and allow to cool until squash can be handled. Scoop the squash out from its skin, keeping the squash skins intact.
4. In a large bowl mix the cooked squash with all of the remaining ingredients plus half a cup of water.
5. Return the mixture to the skins, packing in it firmly.
6. Return the squash halves to the baking sheet, cover loosely with foil, and bake for another 30 minutes.

Serves 4

Calories: 355   **Protein:** 15 grams   **Sugar:** 12 grams
Fat: 8 grams   **Saturated Fat:** 1 gram   **Fiber:** 21 grams
Sodium: 405 mg   **Carbs:** 64 grams

CAULIFLOWER RICE RISOTTO

1 large head cauliflower, about 1 ½ pounds
2 Tb coconut oil
1 onion, chopped
2 garlic cloves, minced
¼ cup pine nuts, toasted
4 oz shiitake mushrooms, sliced
4 oz portabella mushrooms, chopped
8 oz cremini mushrooms, sliced
8 oz asparagus, woody ends removed and cut into ½" pieces
1 Tb vegetable stock base
1 tsp crushed fresh rosemary
½ tsp ground sage
cracked black pepper
2 Tb nutritional yeast flakes

1. Make a vegetable broth by adding the soup base to two cups of simmering water. Keep the broth over a very low flame.
2. Prepare the cauliflower rice by removing the stem and adding the florets to a food processor. Process until finely ground.
3. Heat the oil in a large heavy pan. Sauté the onions and garlic until just starting to brown. Add the pine nuts, mushrooms, and asparagus and cook, stirring, for another minute.
4. Add one cup of the broth and cook, stirring occasionally, for five minutes.
5. Add the cauliflower rice and remaining broth along with the rosemary, sage, and pepper. Cook, uncovered, for ten minutes, or until the cauliflower and asparagus are tender.
6. Remove from heat and stir in the nutritional yeast flakes.

Serves 4

Calories: 250   **Protein:** 12 grams   **Sugar:** 9 grams
Fat: 14 grams   **Saturated Fat:** 7 grams   **Fiber:** 9 grams
Sodium: 452 mg   **Carbs:** 26 grams

CREAMY "PASTA" PRIMAVERA

Coconut cream can be found in health food stores or online. Don't buy cream of coconut as it is loaded with sugar and preservatives.

1 large spaghetti squash, halved lengthwise, seeds removed
2 Tb olive oil
2 medium zucchini, halved and sliced
2 large carrots, halved and sliced
½ red onion, chopped
2 garlic cloves, minced
1 bell pepper, halved and sliced
1 cup fresh or frozen peas
½ cup coconut cream
¼ cup cashew or almond butter
½ ripe avocado, mashed
½ tsp sea salt, plus more for the spaghetti squash
½ tsp dried thyme
cracked black pepper

1. Prepare the spaghetti squash by rubbing the inside with half of the olive oil, then sprinkle with salt and pepper. Bake in a 350°F oven, cut halves up, for an hour. Allow to cool.
2. Meanwhile, heat the remaining tablespoon of oil in a large pan. Sauté the onion, garlic, carrot, and bell pepper for five minutes. Add the zucchini, peas, and thyme and cook for five more minutes. Add the coconut cream, nut butter, and ½ cup water and stir until well mixed with the vegetables.
3. Turn off the heat and add the avocado, salt, and pepper.
4. Once the spaghetti squash is cool enough to handle, use a fork to separate the strands of the squash. Divide the squash "pasta" between four plates and top with the creamy vegetable sauce.

Serves 4

Calories: 425   **Protein:** 10 grams   **Sugar:** 16 grams
Fat: 29 grams   **Saturated Fat:** 12 grams   **Fiber:** 10 grams
Sodium: 410 mg   **Carbs:** 39 grams

STRAWBERRY PASTA

This might sound like a weird combination, but, trust me, it's delicious, and not at all overly sweet. It's incredibly easy to make, but tastes like you spent hours on it. It's best served right away and at room temperature. Chilling it will cause the coconut cream to congeal.

8 oz fresh strawberries
2 Tb extra virgin olive oil
8 oz gluten free pasta
½ cup coconut cream
½ tsp sea salt
¼ cup mint, sliced

1. Cook the pasta according to the package directions.
2. Make the strawberry sauce by blending the strawberries, olive oil, coconut cream, and salt in a blender or food processer.
3. Add the sauce to the cooked pasta.
4. Garnish with the mint.

Serves 4

Calories: 390 **Protein:** 8 grams **Sugar:** 7 grams
Fat: 18 grams **Saturated Fat:** 10 grams **Fiber:** 5 grams
Sodium: 295 mg **Carbs:** 39 grams

ROSEMARY HERB PASTA

4 garlic cloves, crushed
¼ cup olive oil
1 lb gluten free pasta
1 small bunch rosemary, chopped
1 small bunch parsley, chopped
1 small bunch dill, chopped
4 large tomatoes, diced
1 14oz can white beans, like cannellini, drained
1 Tb balsamic vinegar
1 tsp sea salt
cracked black pepper

1. Cook the pasta according to the package directions.
2. Heat the olive oil in a large pot. Add the garlic and cook for one minute before adding the fresh herbs. Stir for another three minutes then turn off the heat.
3. Add the tomatoes, white beans, balsamic, salt, and pepper. Stir until well mixed.
4. Add the pasta and toss to combine.

Serves 8

Calories: 355
Fat: 8 grams
Sodium: 305 mg

Protein: 11 grams
Saturated Fat: 1 gram
Carbs: 58 grams

Sugar: 8 grams
Fiber: 7 grams

MUSHROOM STROGANOFF

This can also be served over gluten-free pasta.

1 lb Portobello mushrooms, cut in ½" slices
4 Tb soy-free vegan margarine
1 onion, chopped
8 oz button mushrooms, sliced
1/8 tsp nutmeg
1 tsp ground sage
1 cup coconut cream
1 tsp sea salt
cracked black pepper
3 cups cooked brown rice

1. Melt half of the margarine in a large heavy pan. Add the Portobello mushrooms and onion and cook until soft, about five minutes. Set aside.
2. In the same pan melt the other two tablespoons of margarine. Add the button mushrooms, nutmeg, and sage. Cook for about five minutes.
3. Turn the heat to low and add the coconut cream, salt, and pepper. Stir well to combine.
4. Add the Portobello mushrooms and simmer until warm.
5. Serve over ½ cup brown rice per serving.

Serves 6

Calories: 330   **Protein:** 7 grams   **Sugar:** 5 grams
Fat: 21 grams   **Saturated Fat:** 15 grams   **Fiber:** 4 grams
Sodium: 458 mg   **Carbs:** 32 grams

6
SIDES

Ah, yet another cookbook chapter I tend to ignore because there is rarely anything noteworthy to be found. Sides are just about the easiest thing to make—sauté some zucchini and serve it with a drizzle of olive oil and cracked black pepper, blanch some asparagus and serve with a squeeze of lemon. You don't need me to tell you how to chop up and heat vegetables.

This was the most difficult chapter for me to write as I didn't want to provide the same things as other books, things that you could probably make with your eyes closed. You don't need another recipe for salsa, guacamole, or tomato sauce. I don't like it when a cookbook boasts "100 recipes" when half of them are for sauces, dips, and sides. I hope I was at least moderately successful with presenting a few newish ideas!

GARLICY PORTOBELLO CAPS

4 large Portobello mushrooms, with stems if possible
2 Tb olive oil
½ small onion
3 garlic cloves, crushed
¼ cup almond meal flour
10 fresh basil leaves
¼ cup pine nuts
½ tsp sea salt

5. Preheat the oven to 350°F.
6. Remove the stems from the mushrooms and set aside.
7. Drizzle half of the olive oil over the undersides of the mushrooms and place them in a baking pan.
8. Place the mushroom stems, onion, garlic, almond meal, and basil leaves in a food processor. Pulse until combined.
9. Add the remaining olive oil and one tablespoon of water. Process until combined. If mixture seems very dry and crumbly, add another tablespoon of water.
10. Add the pine nuts and salt to the garlic mixture.
11. Spread the mixture on top of the mushroom caps.
12. Bake for fifteen minutes, or until the mushrooms are tender and the mixture is browned on top.

Serves 4

Calories: 155
Fat: 13 grams
Sodium: 309 mg

Protein: 4 grams
Saturated Fat: 2 grams
Carbs: 8 grams

Sugar: 3 grams
Fiber: 3 grams

PORCINI CUPS

¼ cup dried porcini mushrooms
1 Tb palm oil
2 shallots, diced
2 garlic cloves, crushed
1 jalapeño, seeded and diced
2 celery stalks, diced
8 oz cremini mushrooms, diced
½ cup almond meal flour
1 Tb fresh parsley, chopped
½ tsp sea salt
cracked black pepper

1. Preheat the oven to 350°F. Grease four individual ramekins.
2. Put the porcini mushrooms in a glass bowl and cover with boiling water. Cover the bowl and allow to sit for 15 minutes, then drain, let cool, and chop.
3. Heat the oil in a pan and add the shallots, jalapeño, garlic, and celery. Sauté for five minutes then add both of the mushrooms to the pan. Cook for five more minutes.
4. Turn off the heat and add the almond meal flour, parsley, salt, and pepper. If it seems crumbly add water to keep the mixture one tablespoon at a time.
5. Divide into the ramekins. Place the dishes in a small baking pan and add boiling water to the pan so it comes half way up the ramekins.
6. Bake for 20 minutes, or until a toothpick inserted in the center comes out clean.
7. Let stand for ten minutes before serving. They can be turned out onto plates or served in the ramekins.

Serves 4

Calories: 150   **Protein:** 5 grams   **Sugar:** 3 grams
Fat: 11 grams   **Saturated Fat:** 2 grams   **Fiber:** 3 grams
Sodium: 322 mg   **Carbs:** 12 grams

COLLARD GREENS

There were many foods I didn't know existed until I moved to New York. Soul food was definitely one of them. I'm including this recipe for all those people living in small towns in the Midwest who have never heard of collards!

3 bunches collard or mustard greens, about 1 ½ pounds
1 large onion, chopped
2 Tb olive oil
4 garlic cloves, crushed
½ tsp crushed red pepper flakes
1 tsp sea salt
1 Tb coconut aminos

1. Remove the stems from the greens and chop.
2. Heat the oil in a large, heavy pan and add the onion, garlic, and red pepper. Cook until the onions are slightly brown.
3. Add the greens, salt, coconut aminos, and one cup of water.
4. Cover and simmer for half an hour, stirring occasionally to make certain the bottom doesn't burn. Add more water if necessary.
5. Remove from heat and add black pepper if desired.

Serves 6

Calories: 100   **Protein:** 4 grams   **Sugar:** 2 grams
Fat: 5 grams   **Saturated Fat:** 1 gram   **Fiber:** 5 grams
Sodium: 531 mg   **Carbs:** 11 grams

SMALL GRAINS PILAF

A gluten-free high-protein take on your usual pilaf dish.

1 cup wild rice, uncooked
1 cup quinoa, uncooked
1 cup millet, uncooked
1 Tb vegetable stock base
1 large onion, chopped
1 clove garlic, minced
1 Tb palm oil
1 tsp dried thyme
1 Tb coconut aminos
1 tsp sea salt
cracked black pepper

1. Bring six cups of water to a boil. Add the wild rice and vegetable stock base. Lower heat, cover, and simmer for fifteen minutes
2. Add the millet. Cover and simmer for fifteen more minutes.
3. Add the quinoa, salt, and pepper. Cover and simmer for fifteen more minutes. Add more water if necessary.
4. Meanwhile, heat the oil in a large, heavy pan and add the onion, garlic, and thyme. Cook until the onions are slightly brown.
5. Add the sautéed mixture to the cooked grains.
6. Remove from heat and add coconut aminos, salt, and pepper.

Serves 12

Calories: 185
Fat: 3 grams
Sodium: 351 mg

Protein: 6 grams
Saturated Fat: 1 gram
Carbs: 34 grams

Sugar: 1 grams
Fiber: 4 grams

KALE COLCANNON

Colcannon is a traditional Irish dish made with potatoes and cabbage or kale. Of course, my version uses sweet potatoes to up the nutrition value and substitutes vegan options for the butter and milk. For a vegetarian version use the traditional dairy ingredients.

4 large sweet potatoes, chopped
2 Tb soy-free vegan margarine, divided
1 cup hemp milk
1 tsp sea salt
cracked black pepper
1 bunch kale, about 1 lb, woody stems removed and chopped
3 scallions, chopped

1. Boil the sweet potatoes until tender.
2. Drain and mash with one tablespoon of margarine, hemp milk, salt, and pepper.
3. Heat the remaining tablespoon of margarine in a large pan and sauté the kale and scallions. Add one tablespoon of water and cover. Lower heat and cook until the kale is soft and wilted, about ten minutes.
4. Add the kale to the potatoes.

Serves 8

Calories: 115   **Protein:** 4 grams   **Sugar:** 4 grams
Fat: 3 grams   **Saturated Fat:** 1 gram   **Fiber:** 4 grams
Sodium: 389 mg   **Carbs:** 19 grams

SAAG

Spinach cooked with Indian spices. The margarine can be replaced with ghee for a more authentic flavor.

2 lbs fresh spinach, washed and thinly sliced
2 Tb soy-free vegan margarine
2 tsp ground cumin
1 small jalapeño, seeded and minced
1 clove garlic, crushed
1 tsp turmeric
2 tsp ground coriander
1 tsp sea salt

1. Heat the margarine in a large pan and add the cumin, pepper, garlic and turmeric.
2. Cook for a minute before adding the spinach. Cook over medium heat, stirring constantly, until spinach starts to wilt.
3. Add the coriander and salt.
4. Lower heat, cover, and simmer for ten minutes.
5. Remove from heat and serve.

Serves 6

Calories: 75   **Protein:** 5 grams   **Sugar:** 1 gram
Fat: 5 grams   **Saturated Fat:** 1 gram   **Fiber:** 4 grams
Sodium: 544 mg   **Carbs:** 7 grams

RED LENTIL DAHL

This can be made with brown lentils, but the red ones result in a smoother texture. As with the saag recipe, the oil can be replaced with ghee.

1 cup red lentils
1 tsp turmeric
1 small onion, diced
1 clove garlic
1 Tb palm oil
1 tsp ground mustard
1 tsp ground ginger
½ small jalapeño, seeded and minced
1 tsp ground cumin
1 tsp ground cardamom
½ tsp sea salt

1. Bring two cups of water to boil. Add the lentils and turmeric, cover and simmer for 15 minutes, or until lentils are tender. Add more water if necessary.
2. Meanwhile sauté the onion and garlic in the palm oil along with the mustard, ginger, pepper, cumin, and cardamom. Cover and simmer for five minutes.
3. Add the sautéed mixture to the cooked lentils along with the salt.

Serves 4

Calories: 215
Fat: 5 grams
Sodium: 298 mg

Protein: 13 grams
Saturated Fat: 2 grams
Carbs: 33 grams

Sugar: 1 gram
Fiber: 6 grams

BLACK BEAN FRITTERS

1 small red bell pepper, finely diced
1 small green bell pepper, finely diced
1 small zucchini, grated
1 ½ cups cooked black beans, drained if canned
½ cup brown rice flour
1 tsp baking powder
2 tsp sea salt
4 Tb coconut oil

1. Combine the bell peppers, zucchini, and black beans in a large bowl. Use a potato masher or the back of a large spoon to mash some of the black beans while leaving others intact. Alternately, you can pulse them in a food processor then add the diced vegetables.
2. Add the flour, baking powder, and salt and mix until fully combined. If the mixture seems thick you can add one or two tablespoons of water.
3. Make small pancakes of the black bean mixture by rolling and lightly flattening ¼ cup at a time.
4. Heat one tablespoon of coconut oil at a time. Cook four fritters at a time, cooking three minutes on each side.
5. Set the cooked fritters on paper towel to absorb the oil.

Makes 16
Per Fritter:

Calories: 75	**Protein:** 2 grams	**Sugar:** 1 gram
Fat: 4 grams	**Saturated Fat:** 3 grams	**Fiber:** 2 grams
Sodium: 178 mg	**Carbs:** 8 grams	

EGGPLANT TABBOULEH

The couscous in tabbouleh can be substituted with quinoa or millet. Millet is fluffier, while quinoa has more protein. This dish can be served room temperature, warm, or chilled.

1 eggplant, diced
2 tsp sea salt
2 cups cooked and cooled quinoa
2 cups cooked and cooled millet
1 large shallot, diced
2 Tb extra virgin olive oil
1 Tb sriracha
1 Tb tahini
¼ cup lemon juice
1 cup mint leaves, chopped
1 cup basil leaves, chopped
1 cup cilantro leaves, chopped

1. Prepare the eggplant by placing it in a colander and sprinkling it with one teaspoon of the sea salt. Let rest for at least an hour. Rinse and set on paper towel to dry, pressing more paper towel on the top to help absorb the liquid.
2. Meanwhile bring one inch of water to boil in a large pot. Place the eggplant in a steam basket and steam with the lid on for five minutes. Remove and let cool.
3. Put the quinoa and millet in a large bowl and allow to cool.
4. In a small bowl combine shallot, olive oil, sriracha, tahini, lemon juice, and remaining teaspoon sea salt. Pour mixture over the grains, stirring well.
5. Fold in the fresh herbs and eggplant.

Serves 8

Calories: 175
Fat: 6 grams
Sodium: 341 mg

Protein: 5 grams
Saturated Fat: 1 gram
Carbs: 27 grams

Sugar: 4 grams
Fiber: 5 grams

BUTTERNUT SQUASH FRIES

This is an alternate from the usual sweet potato fries. I love cutting sweet potatoes into wedges, tossing with olive oil and spices and baking until golden, but sometimes it's nice to have something different every now and then.

1 large butternut squash, about 1 ½ pounds
2 Tb olive oil
½ tsp sea salt
fresh cracked pepper

1. Preheat the oven to 400°F. Line two large baking sheets with parchment paper or foil. If using foil, spray with cooking spray or brush with oil.
2. Prepare the squash by peeling, then cutting in half lengthwise. Scoop out the seeds and discard. Cut the squash in thirds and then slice into ¼" slices.
3. Toss the pieces in the olive oil and spread on the prepared baking sheet. Spring with the salt and pepper.
4. Bake for 45 minutes, turning over halfway through.

Serves 4

Calories: 135   **Protein:** 2 grams   **Sugar:** 4 grams
Fat: 7 grams   **Saturated Fat:** 1 gram   **Fiber:** 3 grams
Sodium: 299 mg   **Carbs:** 20 grams

BAKED BEANS

Baked beans are delicious. We all know this. But canned varieties are laden with sugar, salt, preservatives, and sometimes pork and lard. While they take a while to prepare, the effort is worth the wait.

1 cup dried navy beans, soaked overnight
2 Tb palm oil
1 onion, diced
2 tomatoes, diced
1 Tb blackstrap molasses
1 tsp sea salt

1. Rinse the beans and place with in a pot with freshly boiled water. Cover and simmer for an hour, until beans are very tender. Drain.
2. Preheat the oven to 350°F. Prepare a 8"x8" glass baking dish by coating with cooking spray or rubbing it with oil.
3. Heat the oil in a small pan and sauté the onion until golden.
4. In a large bowl combine the beans, onion, tomato, molasses, and salt.
5. Pour into the prepared baking dish. Bake for one hour, stirring once or twice while baking. If the beans seem dry when you check them, you can add a quarter cup of water while they are still baking.

Serves 6

Calories: 180   **Protein:** 8 grams   **Sugar:** 5 grams
Fat: 5 grams   **Saturated Fat:** 2 grams   **Fiber:** 9 grams
Sodium: 405 mg   **Carbs:** 27 grams

7
SNACKS

JJ Virgin advises her clients to avoid snacking. It makes sense—most people add hundreds of empty calories a day to their diets by mindless eating. But I have a confession to make: I love snacking. Love it! I get home from work and I snack. I finish dinner and then I snack. Going on a road trip? Well, then, I'd better prepare the snacks! And, no, I am not 200 pounds. I just snack smart and exercise daily so that I continue my cherished snack habit.

This chapter contains healthy but not boring snack options so that if you're like me, you don't have to say goodbye to between-meal pleasure.

GRANOLA

I love taking granola with me on long hikes. It's light, yet loaded with tons of energy. Just don't overdo it, as it is also rather calorie dense. You can add dried fruit like raisins or cranberries, or dairy free chocolate chips, to make it a sweeter treat. This makes a loose, flakey granola. If you want it more in bunches, try reducing the oil and increasing the honey, but know that this will add more sugar.

½ cup sesame seeds
½ cup sunflower seeds
¼ cup flax seeds
½ cup unsweetened coconut flakes
1 cup almonds
2 cups old-fashioned oats (like Bob's Red Mill)
½ tsp cinnamon
½ tsp ground cardamom
¼ tsp sea salt
¼ cup raw honey
¼ cup palm oil
1 Tb vanilla extract

1. Preheat the oven to 300°F. Line a large baking pan with parchment paper.
2. Combine the first nine ingredients in the prepared baking pan. Bake, stirring occasionally, for about 30 minutes. Be careful not to burn.
3. Mix the honey, oil, and vanilla extract. Pour it on top of the oat mixture and stir well.
4. Bake for another 30 minutes, watching carefully and stirring occasionally so it doesn't burn.
5. Let cool and divide into snack containers or baggies.

Makes about 6 cups
Per ½ cup serving:

Calories: 310	**Protein:** 8 grams	**Sugar:** 7 grams
Fat: 22 grams	**Saturated Fat:** 6 grams	**Fiber:** 6 grams
Sodium: 55 mg	**Carbs:** 23 grams	

FIG ALMOND BITES

Another travel-friendly snack. This one is raw.

4 cups dried figs, stems removed and quartered
½ tsp cardamom
2 tsp cinnamon
1 Tb raw honey
2 Tb red wine
¾ cup raw almonds, chopped

1. Place the figs, cardamom, cinnamon, honey, and red wine in a food processor and process until well mixed.
2. Add the chopped almonds process until blended.
3. Roll tablespoons of the mixture into little balls.
4. Refrigerate.

Makes about 32 bites
Per bite:

Calories: 60   **Protein:** 1 gram   **Sugar:** 10 grams
Fat: 1 gram   **Saturated Fat:** 0 grams   **Fiber:** 2 grams
Sodium: 2 mg   **Carbs:** 13 grams

COCONUT NUT COOKIES

One of my favorite after work snacks is a nice nutty cookie. These are fairly low in sugar.

1 cup almond flour
½ cup coconut flour
1 tsp baking soda
½ cup all-purpose gluten-free flour (like Bob's Red Mill)
½ tsp xanthan gum
½ tsp sea salt
¼ cup xylitol
¼ cup unsweetened apple sauce
1 tsp vanilla
¼ cup raw honey
½ cup chopped nuts of choice—try pecan or macadamias
¼ cup shredded unsweetened coconut

1. Preheat the oven to 350°F. Line a cookie sheet with parchment paper.
2. In a large bowl mix the flours, baking soda, xanthan gum, salt, and xylitol.
3. In a separate bowl combine the apple sauce, vanilla, and honey.
4. Add the liquid to the flour mixture, then mix in the nuts and shredded coconut.
5. Divide into 12 parts. Roll into balls and flatten on the cookie sheet. Bake for 15 to 20 minutes, or until golden brown.

Makes 12 large cookies
Per cookie:

Calories: 160	**Protein:** 4 grams	**Sugar:** 7 grams
Fat: 9 grams	**Saturated Fat:** 2 grams	**Fiber:** 4 grams
Sodium: 216 mg	**Carbs:** 18 grams	

BAKED ARTICHOKE DIP

This is fabulous with gluten-free crackers or crudités.

1 green bell pepper, diced
1 red bell pepper, diced
1 celery stalk, diced
2 Tb palm oil, divided
2 Tb brown mustard
2 Tb apple cider vinegar
½ tsp sea salt
1 14oz can artichoke hearts or bottoms, drained and chopped
1 jalapeño pepper, seeded and diced
2 scallions, chopped
2 Tb nutritional yeast flakes
2 Tb lemon juice
1 tsp sriracha sauce
¼ cup sliced almonds

1. Preheat the oven to 350°F.
2. Heat one tablespoon of the oil in a pan. Sauté the bell peppers until soft and tender.
3. In a large bowl combine all of the remaining ingredients except the almonds. Add the cooked bell peppers and the remaining tablespoon of oil.
4. Pour the mixture into an 8"x8" glass baking dish. Top with the almonds.
5. Bake for 25 minutes, or until brown on top.

Serves 8

Calories: 95
Fat: 5 grams
Sodium: 343 mg

Protein: 4 grams
Saturated Fat: 2 grams
Carbs: 10 grams

Sugar: 2 grams
Fiber: 4 grams

ARTICHOKE BRUSCHETTA

2 garlic cloves, minced
½ tsp sea salt
cracked black pepper
1 14oz can artichoke hearts or bottoms, drained and chopped
2 Tb olive oil
8 pitted kalamata olives, chopped
4 plum tomatoes, chopped
2 Tb fresh parsley, chopped
2 Tb capers, drained
4 slices gluten-free bread, halved and toasted

1. Place the garlic, salt, pepper, artichokes, and oil in a food processor. Pulse until well blended.
2. Turn the puréed mixture into a bowl and add the remaining ingredients except for the bread. If the mixture contains too much liquid, drain it in a colander before serving.
3. Top each slice of toasted bread with the artichoke mixture.

Makes 8
Per piece:

Calories: 95   **Protein:** 3 grams   **Sugar:** 2 grams
Fat: 5 grams   **Saturated Fat:** 1 gram   **Fiber:** 3 grams
Sodium: 356 mg   **Carbs:** 12 grams

SAVORY PUMPKIN MUFFINS

These aren't sweet morning muffins. The sage adds a bit of complexity to these muffins. Most canned pumpkin doesn't contain added sugar, but check the label. Don't buy pumpkin pie filling, though! You can also cook and mash your own pumpkin.

1 cup all-purpose gluten-free flour, like Bob's Red Mill
1 ½ cups almond flour
¼ cup potato starch
¼ cup tapioca starch
1 tsp baking soda
½ tsp sea salt
2 Tb raw honey
2 Tb coconut oil
½ cup unsweetened coconut milk
1 cup pumpkin
½ tsp dried ground sage

1. Preheat the oven to 350°F. Line a muffin pan with baking cups.
2. In a large bowl whisk together the flours, starches, baking soda, and salt.
3. In a smaller bowl combine the honey, oil, milk, pumpkin, and sage.
4. Mix the wet into the dry ingredients until fully combined.
5. Spoon into the prepared baking cups.
6. Bake for 30 minutes, or until lightly browned and a toothpick inserted in the center comes out clean.

Makes 12
Per muffin:

Calories: 175
Fat: 10 grams
Sodium: 210 mg

Protein: 4 grams
Saturated Fat: 3 grams
Carbs: 20 grams

Sugar: 4 grams
Fiber: 3 grams

WHITE BEAN HUMMUS

This is good for when you're bored of the usual hummus dip.

1 14oz can white beans, like cannellini, drained
¼ cup tahini
2 Tb lemon juice
2 Tb extra virgin olive oil
1 garlic clove, crushed
½ tsp ground cumin
½ tsp sea salt
cracked black pepper

1. Combine all of the ingredients in a food processor.
2. Blend until smooth. Add one or two tablespoons of water if a thinner consistency is desired.
3. Serve with crudités or gluten-free crackers.

Makes about 2 cups
Per ¼ cup serving:

Calories: 135　　**Protein:** 5 grams　　**Sugar:** 0 grams
Fat: 8 grams　　**Saturated Fat:** 1 gram　　**Fiber:** 3 grams
Sodium: 158 mg　　**Carbs:** 13 grams

PLANTAIN CHIPS AND BLACK BEAN DIP

I love plantain chips, but store-bought ones are fried. Be sure to use green plantains—this doesn't work with ripe, yellow ones. Also, use parchment paper, not foil, as they will stick to the foil.

2 green plantains
2 Tb olive oil, divided
1 tsp sea salt, divided
1 onion, chopped
2 garlic cloves, crushed
3 cups cooked black beans, rinsed if canned
1 tsp ground cumin
¼ tsp cayenne pepper
1 large tomato, diced
¼ cup cilantro, chopped

1. Preheat the oven to 400°F. Line two large cooking sheets with parchment baking paper.
2. Peel the plantains and slice very thin with a mandolin. Toss them with half the olive oil and Spread them in a single layer on the baking sheet. Sprinkle with half of the salt and bake for 20 minutes.
3. Meanwhile prepare the dip. Heat the remaining tablespoon of oil in a skillet and sauté the onion and garlic until golden.
4. Put the sautéed vegetables in a food processor along with the black beans, cumin, remaining salt, and cayenne. Process until smooth. Add a few tablespoons of water if the mixture seems too thick.
5. Stir in the tomato and cilantro.

Serves 6

Calories: 220
Fat: 3 grams
Sodium: 396 mg

Protein: 9 grams
Saturated Fat: 1 gram
Carbs: 43 grams

Sugar: 11 grams
Fiber: 10 grams

CHOCOLATE NUT BUTTER POPSICLES

Before you protest the idea of a popsicle as a snack, I think they are an ideal summer snack at any time of day, not just dessert. I use a Zoku popsicle maker, but the old fashion plastic ones work just fine.

¼ cup raw honey
3 Tb xylitol
¼ cup nut butter of choice, I generally use almond
1 oz dark chocolate, at least 70% cocoa, chopped
¼ tsp sea salt
⅔ cup unsweetened almond milk
½ tsp apple cider vinegar

1. Bring one cup water to a boil in a small sauce pan.
2. Turn heat off and whisk in the honey, xylitol, nut butter, chocolate, and sea salt. Stir until the nut butter and chocolate are completely melted and xylitol and sea salt are dissolved.
3. Add the almond milk and vinegar.
4. Place the mixture in the refrigerator for an hour to allow it to cool completely.
5. Stir, pour into popsicle molds, and freeze until set.

Makes 9
Per popsicle:

Calories: 100   **Protein:** 2 grams   **Sugar:** 8 grams
Fat: 5 grams   **Saturated Fat:** 1 gram   **Fiber:** 1 gram
Sodium: 77 mg   **Carbs:** 12 grams

GREEN MELON POPSICLES

And one more popsicle recipe, this time something a bit more refreshing. This also works well with different fruits, like peaches or watermelons.

1 Tb raw honey
2 Tb xylitol
1 Tb lime juice
8 oz honeydew melon, chopped
2 mint leaves
½ tsp vanilla extract
¼ cup unsweetened coconut milk

1. Process all of the ingredients in a blender until completely liquefied. Add another tablespoon or two of coconut milk if needed.
2. Pour into popsicle molds and freeze until set.

Makes 6
Per popsicle:

Calories: 40   **Protein:** 0 grams   **Sugar:** 6 grams
Fat: 0 grams   **Saturated Fat:** 0 grams   **Fiber:** 0 grams
Sodium: 8 mg   **Carbs:** 9 grams

8
DESSERTS

For someone who loves snacking, I'm not that big into dessert. That's because I prefer savory and salty flavors to sweet ones. My partner, however, has a massive sweet tooth, so I regularly prepare sweet treats for him. Dessert doesn't need to be a no-no if you're mindful about how much sugar you're consuming and keep proportions reasonable.

BROWN RICE PUDDING

The tiny amount of low-glycemic molasses in this recipe won't send you into a sugar crash, plus molasses is an excellent source of iron, folic acid, magnesium, calcium, and other amazing minerals like copper and zinc! The raisins plump upon cooking.

⅓ cup brown rice
¼ cup blackstrap molasses
¼ tsp sea salt
¼ cup raisins
2 tsp vanilla extract
3 cups unsweetened coconut milk
1 Tb brandy

1. Preheat oven to 350°F.
2. Grease a 8"x8" glass baking dish.
3. Combine all of the ingredients except the brandy in a large bowl.
4. Pour into the prepared baking dish.
5. Bake for about two hours, stirring every 20 minutes to prevent the formation of a skin.
6. After an hour and a half add the brandy.
7. It should still seem soft when you remove it from the oven. It will thicken some as it cools.

Serves 6

Calories: 125   **Protein:** 2 grams   **Sugar:** 11 grams
Fat: 3 grams   **Saturated Fat:** 2 grams   **Fiber:** 1 gram
Sodium: 148 mg   **Carbs:** 22 grams

KHEER

This is the dessert my partner is always asking me to make. Kheer is an Indian rice pudding that is a bit runnier than a traditional rice pudding. If you want a richer version, used canned coconut milk, light or full fat, depending on how much you want to indulge.

4 cups unsweetened coconut milk
½ cup brown Basmati or jasmine rice
1 tsp ground cardamom
¼ cup slivered almonds
¼ cup pistachios, chopped
¼ tsp sea salt
¼ cup raw honey

1. In a large pot, bring the coconut milk, rice, and honey to a boil.
2. Lower the heat and simmer for half an hour, stirring occasionally.
3. Add the cardamom, almonds, pistachios, and salt. Cook for another 30 minutes, or until it is slightly thickened. It will continue to thicken upon refrigeration, but should still remain creamy
4. Chill and refrigerate for at least an hour before serving. This can also be served warm or room temperature.

Serves 6

Calories: 180
Fat: 8 grams
Sodium: 103 mg

Protein: 4 grams
Saturated Fat: 3 grams
Carbs: 26 grams

Sugar: 9 grams
Fiber: 2 grams

APPLE CRANBERRY CRUMBLE

I love a nice fruit crumble. Really, any fruits can be used in this recipe, so feel free to experiment. Another favorite combination of mine is rhubarb and strawberry.

4 apples, cored and chopped
1 ½ cups unsweetened apple cider
1 tsp cinnamon
1 tsp cardamom
2 cups cranberries
2 Tb arrowroot
½ cup almonds
¼ cup walnuts
½ cup old-fashioned oats
¼ cup coconut flour
¼ tsp baking powder
¼ tsp baking soda
½ cup xylitol
1 Tb coconut oil
1 tsp vanilla extract

1. Preheat oven to 350°F. Grease a glass casserole dish.
2. Simmer the apples in a large pot with the cider, cinnamon, and cardamom. Stew for five minutes before adding the cranberries. Cover and simmer for ten minutes.
3. Turn off the heat and whisk in the arrowroot, careful not to let lumps form. Pour into the prepared baking pan.
4. Make the crumble topping by combining the remaining ingredients along with one or two tablespoons of water in a food processor and pulsing until combined but not mushy.
5. Sprinkle the topping over the fruit and bake for 30 minutes, or until the top is lightly browned.

Serves 8

Calories: 250 **Protein:** 4 grams **Sugar:** 16 grams
Fat: 10 grams **Saturated Fat:** 3 grams **Fiber:** 7 grams
Sodium: 62 mg **Carbs:** 39 grams

PERSIMMON SORBET

I love my Cuisinart ice cream maker. I highly recommend it for anyone who wants to make healthy ice creams and fruit sorbets. This is another recipe that is easily adapted to other fruits, like peaches and nectarines. Persimmons are subtly sweet and buttery smooth. They're easiest to find in autumn. The xanthan gum and vodka aren't necessary, but they keep the sorbet from freezing rock hard when stored in the freezer.

If you don't have an ice cream maker, pout the mixture into a freezer safe container with a lid and stir every half hour for three hours.

5 ripe persimmons
2 Tb raw honey
1 Tb lemon juice
¼ tsp sea salt
¼ tsp powdered ginger
¼ cup mango nectar
1 Tb coconut oil, melted
½ tsp xanthan gum
2 Tb vodka

1. Puree all of the ingredients in a blender until smooth.
2. Pour into the running ice cream maker.
3. Run the ice cream maker for 25 to 45 minutes, depending on how firm you like your sorbet.
4. Serve immediately and freeze leftovers in an airtight container.

Makes 6 cups
Per one cup serving:

Calories: 150   **Protein:** 1 gram   **Sugar:** 24 grams
Fat: 3 grams   **Saturated Fat:** 2 gram   **Fiber:** 5 grams
Sodium: 100 mg   **Carbs:** 33 grams

CHOCOLATE PUDDING

This avocado based pudding is surprisingly good, but it's also very rich, so indulge only occasionally! The portions are rather generous, and it's so rich that I can usually eat only half a serving, so this could easily be made to serve four smaller portions. Earth Balance makes a nice coconut butter spread.

1 ripe avocado
¼ cup cocoa powder
¼ cup unsweetened coconut milk
1 tsp coconut oil, melted
1 Tb coconut butter, melted
2 Tb stevia or xylitol
1 tsp vanilla extract

1. Combine all of the ingredients in a food processor and blend until smooth.
2. Refrigerate for half an hour before serving.

Serves 2

Calories: 220
Fat: 20 grams
Sodium: 45 mg

Protein: 4 grams
Saturated Fat: 7 grams
Carbs: 13 grams

Sugar: 1 gram
Fiber: 8 grams

POACHED PEARS

This elegant desert is surprisingly simple to prepare and always manages to impress.

4 ripe but firm pears, preferably Bosc
2 Tb lemon juice
1 Tb raw honey
2 cinnamon sticks
4 ¼" slices of fresh ginger root
4 whole cloves
1 bay leaf
4 whole peppercorns
4 cardamom pods, bruised

1. Peel the pears, leaving the stalks on, and stand them up in a large bowl or pot. Cut a slice off the bottoms if needed to make them stand.
2. Pour the lemon juice over the pears then add enough water to cover the pears.
3. Bring 1 ¼ cups water to boil in a 2-qt soup pot with a lid. Add the remaining ingredients, cover and simmer for five minutes.
4. Drain the pears and add them to the simmering pot with the spiced syrup. Cover and simmer for 15 minutes. Turn off the heat and allow the pears to cool in the liquid.
5. Remove the pears and place them upright in four serving bowls.
6. Bring the spiced syrup back to a boil and boil, uncovered, for ten minutes, or until the liquid is reduced by half. Pour over the pears.

Serves 4

Calories: 125
Fat: 0 grams
Sodium: 6 mg

Protein: 1 gram
Saturated Fat: 0 grams
Carbs: 34 grams

Sugar: 22 grams
Fiber: 6 grams

BERRY TRIFLE

A vegan version of the delicious dessert well-known in England but often ignored stateside. This is rather calorie dense, so if you like, you can make 16 mini trifles by doing only one layer instead of two. Alternatively, a large trifle can be made by using a large serving bowl instead of individual dishes.

1 cup walnuts
1 cup cashews
6 dates, pits removed
¼ cup unsweetened shredded coconut
4 Tb raw honey, divided
¼ tsp sea salt
1 cup cashews, soaked overnight
1 cup coconut cream
1 tsp vanilla
1 lb fresh strawberries, sliced
12 oz fresh blueberries

1. Preheat the oven to 350°F. Line a cookie sheet with baking parchment.
2. Put the walnuts and unsoaked cashews in a food processor and chop until fine. Add the dates, coconut, 2 Tb honey, salt, and one tablespoon water. Process until sticky.
3. Divide the mixture into 16 balls. Flatten on the prepared cookie sheet and bake for 15 minutes. Allow to cool.
4. Drain the soaked cashews and blend in a food processer with the coconut cream, vanilla, and remaining 2 Tb honey. Refrigerate for at least an hour to allow it to set.
5. To assemble the trifle place a nut cookie at the bottom of a serving dish. Place a layer of berries on the cookie followed by a dollop of the cashew cream. Repeat once more.

Serves 8

Calories: 480 **Protein:** 10 grams **Sugar:** 23 grams
Fat: 36 grams **Saturated Fat:** 14 grams **Fiber:** 6 grams
Sodium: 81 mg **Carbs:** 38 grams

CHOCOLATE TRUFFLES

Don't overdo it on these—remember you're allowed one ounce of dark chocolate a day, not the entire bar! Some almond pastes contain wheat, so be sure to read the label. You could substitute marzipan, but it has more sugar.

4 oz dark chocolate, at least 70% cocoa
3 oz gluten-free almond paste
½ Tb strong hot coffee
½ Tb hazelnut liqueur, like Frangelico
2 Tb unsweetened cocoa powder

1. Break the chocolate into pieces and place in a food processor. Process until finely chopped.
2. Add the marzipan and process until smooth.
3. With the motor running, add the coffee and liqueur. Process until the mixture forms a large ball.
4. Refrigerate for ten minutes until it is firm enough to roll out.
5. Roll one rounded teaspoon of mixture at a time and set on wax paper.
6. Put the cocoa powder in a plastic baggie. Add the rolled truffles and shake gently to coat with cocoa powder.
7. Place the truffles in mini muffin cups and chill in the refrigerator.

Makes 18
Per truffle:

Calories: 60   **Protein:** 1 gram   **Sugar:** 3 grams
Fat: 4 grams   **Saturated Fat:** 2 grams   **Fiber:** 1 gram
Sodium: 2 mg   **Carbs:** 6 grams

RHUBARB TARTS

This could also be altered to make a single larger pie. While the fat content is a bit high, there is very little sugar, which actually has a much bigger impact on our waistlines.

2 cups almond flour
1 stick vegan margarine, cold, diced into small cubes
1 tsp vanilla extract
1 Tb lemon zest
8 oz fresh strawberries, chopped
8 oz fresh rhubarb, chopped
2 Tb raw honey
¼ cup unsweetened shredded coconut
1 Tb lemon juice

1. Prepare the dough by combining the almond flour, cut up margarine, vanilla, and lemon zest in a food processor. Process until a ball forms. This can also be done by hand.
2. Remove the dough, wrap in plastic, and chill in the refrigerator for at least one hour.
3. Meanwhile in a large bowl combine the strawberries, rhubarb, honey, coconut, and lemon juice. Let set.
4. Preheat the oven to 300°F. Line a baking sheet with parchment paper.
5. Remove the dough from the refrigerator and separate into eight parts. Roll into balls and flatten into disks on the prepared baking sheet. Press the center and pull up on the edges to make a hollow space in the center of each disk.
6. Spoon the fruit mixture into the hollows. Shape the edges to hold in the fruit.
7. Bake for 40 minutes.

Makes 8
Per tart:

Calories: 290   **Protein:** 7 grams   **Sugar:** 7 grams
Fat: 25 grams   **Saturated Fat:** 6 grams   **Fiber:** 5 grams
Sodium: 98 mg   **Carbs:** 15 grams

LEMON COOKIES

1 ½ cups almond flour
6 Tb soy-free vegan margarine
¼ cup raw honey
1 tsp vanilla extract
1 Tb lemon zest

1. Preheat the oven to 350°F. Line a baking sheet with parchment paper.
2. Combine all of the ingredients in a food processor and mix until a sticky ball forms.
3. Divide the dough into twelve equal parts and roll each part into a ball. Flatten with a fork on the prepared baking sheet.
4. Bake for 15 to 20 minutes, until lightly browned. Cool completely before serving.

Makes 12 large cookies
Per cookie:

Calories: 140
Fat: 12 grams
Sodium: 43 mg

Protein: 3 grams
Saturated Fat: 2 grams
Carbs: 9 grams

Sugar: 6 grams
Fiber: 2 grams

MACADAMIA NUT COOKIES

While the nuts make these a bit high in fat, there is almost no sugar. Recent studies have shown that sugar is what makes us fat, not fat! So don't feel bad about having one of these cookies after dinner.

1 cup macadamia nuts, finely chopped
1 ¼ cups almond flour
½ tsp baking soda
3 Tb soy-free vegan margarine, melted and divided
1 Tb raw honey
¼ tsp cinnamon

1. Preheat the oven to 350°F. Line a baking sheet with parchment paper.
2. Combine the nuts, almond flour, baking soda, two tablespoons of the melted margarine, and two tablespoons of water. If it seems too crumbly add another tablespoon of water.
3. Divide the mixture into twelve equal parts. Press down to flatten on the baking sheet.
4. Bake for 15 minutes, until lightly browned.
5. Meanwhile combine the remaining tablespoon of margarine, honey, and cinnamon. Brush onto the cookies. Return to the oven and bake for another two minutes.

Makes 12 cookies
Per cookie:

Calories: 170   **Protein:** 3 grams   **Sugar:** 2 grams
Fat: 17 grams   **Saturated Fat:** 3 grams   **Fiber:** 2 grams
Sodium: 78 mg   **Carbs:** 6 grams

9
SEAFOOD DISHES

As I stated in the introduction, I eat seafood once, sometimes twice, a week. I worry about over-fishing and the levels of antibiotics used in farm fishing, so I regularly research which fish are being raised in a safe manner and being caught at a sustainable rate. I began eating seafood as a protein alternative to soy, plus it was the one animal-based food that I missed! I do not, however, want to contribute to pollution or destruction of eco-systems, so I try to stay informed about the best seafood choices.

At the time of this publication, these were the sustainability ratings for seafood readily available on the East Coast:

Best Choice
- Wild Alaskan black cod
- Wild Pacific halibut
- Farm-raised catfish
- Wild striped bass
- Farm-raised striped bass
- Wild Spanish mackerel
- Wild Alaskan salmon
- Live wild lobster
- Wild steamer clams
- Farm-raised bluepoint oysters

- Farm-raised kumamoto oysters

Good Alternative
- Wild bluefish
- Wild flounder
- Wild monkfish
- Farm-raised salmon
- Wild Atlantic Pollock
- Wild Chilean sea bass
- Wild gray sole
- Wild lemon sole
- Wild snapper
- Wild swordfish
- Wild rock shrimp
- Wild cold water lobster tails
- Wild snow crab
- Wild Alaskan king crab
- Wild dry sea scallops
- Wild cherrystone clams
- Wild littleneck clams

On the Path to Sustainability
- Organic farm-raised salmon
- Farm-raised Atlantic salmon
- Farm-raised shrimp

Avoid
- Wild black sea bass
- Farm-raised tilapia
- Canned crabmeat
- Salt cod

Not Yet Rated
- Wild mahi-mahi
- Wild cod
- Wild Pacific halibut

- Branzino
- Farm-raised royal dorade
- Wild tuna (yellowfin, albacore, and bigeye)
- Wild Patagonian red shrimp
- BeauSoleil oysters
- Farm-raised malpeque oysters
- Farm-raised Newfoundland oysters
- Farm-raised Prince Edward Island mussels

For those of you who are concerned about mercury levels in seafood, below is a list of lower-mercury seafood:

- Tilapia
- Salmon
- Lemon sole
- Gray sole
- Flounder
- Cod
- Oysters
- Shrimp
- Clams
- Scallops
- Crab
- Mussels
- Catfish

SMOKED SALMON TOMATO CUPS

Serve these with steamed asparagus and a side salad for a lovely weekend brunch. The smoked salmon is rather salty, so extra salt is generally not needed.

4 large beefsteak tomatoes
4 oz smoked salmon, chopped
1 zucchini, diced
1 Tb palm oil
snipped fresh chives for garnish
cracked black pepper

1. Preheat the broiler.
2. Cut the top off the tomatoes and carefully scoop out flesh and seeds. Chop the flesh and place in a colander for the extra juices to drain. Set the tomato shells upside down on paper towel to drain.
3. Heat the oil in a pan and sauté the zucchini for a few minutes.
4. Add the smoked salmon pieces and chopped tomato flesh. Cook for a few more minutes, until heated.
5. Place the halved tomatoes under the broiler for three minutes to warm them. Careful not to overcook them as they will fall apart if allowed to get too soft.
6. Divide the salmon mixture among the tomato shells. Top with chives and black pepper.

Serves 4

Calories: 105
Fat: 5 grams
Sodium: 235 mg

Protein: 7 grams
Saturated Fat: 2 grams
Carbs: 9 grams

Sugar: 6 grams
Fiber: 3 grams

SALMON NOODLE SOUP

Poaching salmon makes it wonderfully moist and tender. Most soba noodles are made with a combination of wheat and buckwheat flours. Be sure to buy noodles made with 100% buckwheat, or with a combination of buckwheat and another gluten-free ingredient, like sweet potato. This soup does not store well—the noodles tend to clump together at the bottom, so it's best served right away.

1 lb wild salmon fillets, skinned
1 tsp chopped ginger
4 oz shiitake mushroom, stems removed and sliced
4 oz soba noodles, broken in half
8 oz bok choy, chopped
½ tsp red pepper flakes
2 Tb coconut aminos
4 scallions, sliced

1. Bring six cups of water to a boil and add the salmon, mushrooms, and ginger.
2. Simmer, uncovered, for about five minutes, until the salmon starts to flake and break apart.
3. Add the noodles, bok choy, and red pepper flakes. Simmer for another five minutes, or until the noodles are tender.
4. Remove from heat and add the coconut aminos and scallions.

Serves 4

Calories: 290   **Protein:** 28 grams   **Sugar:** 3 grams
Fat: 8 grams   **Saturated Fat:** 1 gram   **Fiber:** 3 grams
Sodium: 598 mg   **Carbs:** 27 grams

GREEN TEA SHRIMP AND RICE SOUP

3 green tea bags
1 stalk lemongrass, sliced
4 oz shiitake mushrooms, sliced
8 oz cleaned shrimp
1 cup cooked brown or wild rice
1 tsp vegetable stock base
¼ tsp sea salt
cracked black pepper
1 Tb sesame oil
4 scallions, sliced
¼ cup cilantro, chopped

1. Bring six cups of water to a simmer. Add the tea bags and lemongrass. Turn off heat and steep for ten minutes. Remove the tea bags and lemongrass and discard them.
2. Turn the heat back on and add the mushrooms, vegetable base, salt, pepper, and shrimp.
3. Simmer for five minutes before adding the brown rice, sesame oil, and scallions.
4. Turn off heat and add the cilantro.

Serves 4

Calories: 170
Fat: 5 grams
Sodium: 514 mg

Protein: 14 grams
Saturated Fat: 1 gram
Carbs: 17 grams

Sugar: 1 gram
Fiber: 2 grams

SALMON AMARANTH SOUP

1 cup uncooked amaranth
8 oz cremini mushrooms, sliced
1 Tb vegetable stock base
2 Tb tomato paste
1 tsp dried thyme
8 oz carrots, chopped
1 Tb coconut aminos
1 lb salmon fillets, skin removed
cracked black pepper
2 Tb dried parsley

1. Bring six cups of water to simmer in a large soup pot or Dutch oven. Add the first seven ingredients. Cover and simmer until the amaranth is tender, about 20 minutes.
2. Add the salmon and simmer, uncovered, for five more minutes.
3. Remove from heat and add the black pepper and parsley.

Serves 6

Calories: 270
Fat: 7 grams
Sodium: 375 mg

Protein: 22 grams
Saturated Fat: 1 gram
Carbs: 29 grams

Sugar: 4 grams
Fiber: 4 grams

WARM SEAFOOD SALAD

1 Tb palm oil
1 jalapeño pepper, seeded and diced
4 oz snow peas, trimmed
6 scallions, chopped
8 oz scallops
8 oz cleaned shrimp
1 large carrot, grated
5 oz mixed baby greens
¼ cup cilantro, chopped
¼ cup basic vinaigrette or dressing of choice

1. Heat oil in a large, heavy pan. Add the pepper and snow peas and sauté for two minutes.
2. Add the scallions, scallops, and shrimp. Continue to sauté until the shrimp and scallops are opaque, about another four minutes.
3. Turn off the heat and add the grated carrot and cilantro.
4. Divide the greens between four plates. Top with the warm seafood mixture and drizzle with vinaigrette.

Serves 4

Calories: 225
Fat: 10 grams
Sodium: 568 mg

Protein: 25 grams
Saturated Fat: 3 grams
Carbs: 10 grams

Sugar: 3 grams
Fiber: 2 grams

GINGER SHRIMP ROLLS

This is nice, light, summer lunch dish. It's perfect for hot days as it can be eaten warm, room temperature, or chilled.

2 carrots, cut into matchsticks
2 celery stalks, cut into matchsticks
2 cucumbers, cut into matchsticks
2 red bell peppers, cut into matchsticks
large romaine lettuce leaves
2 garlic cloves, crushed
1 Tb palm oil
1 jalapeño pepper, seeded and diced
2 Tb fresh ginger
1 Tb lime juice
1 lb cleaned shrimp
¼ cup cilantro, chopped

1. Put the cut vegetables and lettuce leaves on a large serving platter and set aside.
2. Heat the oil in a large heavy pan. Add the garlic, pepper, and ginger. Sauté for two minutes.
3. Add the shrimp and cook for another four minutes, or until the shrimp are no longer pink and are cooked through. Turn off the heat and add the lime juice and cilantro.
4. Divide the shrimp between four plates. Top a lettuce leaf with vegetables of choice, add shrimp, wrap and enjoy.

Serves 4

Calories: 230
Fat: 6 grams
Sodium: 219 mg

Protein: 26 grams
Saturated Fat: 2 grams
Carbs: 18 grams

Sugar: 8 grams
Fiber: 5 grams

LEMON SOLE WITH ORANGE SAUCE

This is a wonderfully tender, flaky fish dish. Serve with salad for a low-calorie, high-protein meal. If you want to make this sound fancy, call it *poisson à l'orange*.

4 6oz wild lemon sole fillets
1 tsp fresh ginger
1 garlic clove, crushed
1 Tb grated orange peel
¼ cup orange juice, no sugar added
1 tsp coconut aminos
1 Tb olive oil

1. Prepare a shallow metal baking dish by lining it with foil and coating it with cooking spray or rubbing it with oil.
2. Place the fish in the prepared baking dish.
3. Combine the remaining ingredients in a bowl and pour it over the fish. Allow the fish to marinade in the refrigerator for at least half an hour.
4. Preheat the broiler.
5. Leave the fish in the marinade pan and broil for five to six minutes, or until cooked through.

Serves 4

Calories: 160   **Protein:** 21 grams   **Sugar:** 1 gram
Fat: 7 grams   **Saturated Fat:** 1 gram   **Fiber:** 0 grams
Sodium: 532 mg   **Carbs:** 3 grams

SIMPLE WHITE FISH

This basic dish allows the fish to shine. My favorite fish to use in this recipe is cod, but any white flaky fish is good.

4 6oz white fillets, like tilapia, sole, or cod
2 Tb olive oil
1 lemon, thinly sliced
1 lemon, cut into wedges
¼ cup dry white wine
½ tsp sea salt
cracked black pepper
2 Tb fresh parsley, chopped

1. Preheat the oven to 350°F.
2. Prepare a shallow metal baking dish by lining it with foil and coating it with cooking spray or rubbing it with oil.
3. Place the fish in the prepared baking dish.
4. Sprinkle with salt and pepper. Drizzle the olive oil on top then layer the lemon slices on the fish, about two slices per fillet. Pour the white wine around the fish.
5. Bake for twenty minutes.
6. Remove from the oven. Discard the lemon slices. Sprinkle with parsley and serve with the lemon wedges.

Serves 4

Calories: 245　　**Protein:** 35 grams　　**Sugar:** 1 gram
Fat: 10 grams　　**Saturated Fat:** 2 grams　　**Fiber:** 1 gram
Sodium: 383 mg　　**Carbs:** 4 grams

HONEY PEPPER SALMON

A different take on salmon. Be sure to buy a high quality brown mustard that doesn't contain high fructose corn syrup or sugar.

4 6oz wild Alaskan salmon fillets
2 Tb olive oil
1 Tb raw honey
2 garlic cloves, minced
2 Tb Dijon mustard
½ tsp cayenne pepper
2 Tb lemon juice
2 Tb fresh dill, chopped
1 lemon, cut into wedges

1. Prepare a shallow metal baking dish by lining it with foil and coating it with cooking spray or rubbing it with oil.
2. Place the fish in the prepared baking dish.
3. Prepare the topping by combining the honey, olive oil, garlic, mustard, pepper, and lemon juice.
4. Brush on the top of the salmon fillets. Allow to marinate for 30 minutes in the refrigerator.
5. Preheat the oven to 350°F. Bake for twenty minutes.
6. Sprinkle with dill and serve with the lemon wedges.

Serves 4

Calories: 330
Fat: 18 grams
Sodium: 256 mg

Protein: 34 grams
Saturated Fat: 3 grams
Carbs: 7 grams

Sugar: 5 grams
Fiber: 1 gram

SCALLOP SKEWERS

These are best cooked on the grill, but can also be cooked under the broiler. If you're on a budget, substitute large shrimp for the scallops.

2 large zucchini, sliced into ½" rounds
2 14oz jars artichoke bottoms
1 lb scallops
1 Tb extra virgin olive oil
1 Tb lime juice
¼ tsp cayenne pepper
1 clove garlic, minced

1. Combine the oil, lime juice, pepper, and garlic in a one-quart plastic baggie. Add the scallops and allow to marinate for at least 15 minutes.
2. If using wooden skewers, soak them for at least 15 minutes.
3. Make the skewers by alternating the zucchini, artichokes, and scallops—each skewer should have at least two pieces of each.
4. Brush with the marinade.
5. Cook over hot coals or under a preheated broiler, turning once, until the scallops are finished, about 6 minutes on each side.

Makes 8
Per skewer:

Calories: 125   **Protein:** 16 grams   **Sugar:** 1 gram
Fat: 2 grams   **Saturated Fat:** 0 grams   **Fiber:** 4 grams
Sodium: 477 mg   **Carbs:** 11 grams

THAI FISH CAKES

If you can't find lime leaves, use a tablespoon of grated lime peel. If Thai chilies are hard to find, use half of one small jalapeño. These are really good served with the Creamy Moroccan Dressing on page 44.

1 lb boneless white fish, finely chopped
1 Thai chili, seeded and diced
1 Tb raw honey
1 Tb fish sauce
4 lime leaves, chopped
1 small red bell pepper, diced
2 Tb coconut oil

1. Place all the ingredients except the coconut oil into a food processor and blend until smooth but there are still visible pieces of bell pepper.
2. Divide into eight parts and roll into balls. Flatten into patties.
3. Heat one tablespoon of oil in a large pan. Cook four patties until brown on each side, about four minutes per side.
4. Repeat with the remaining oil and patties. Set patties on paper towel to absorb some of the cooking oil before serving.

Makes 8
Per fish cake:

Calories: 120 **Protein:** 11 grams **Sugar:** 3 grams
Fat: 7 grams **Saturated Fat:** 2 grams **Fiber:** 1 gram
Sodium: 207 mg **Carbs:** 3 grams

RED SNAPPER WITH AVOCADO CREAM

4 6oz red snapper fillets
1 cup dry white wine
2 Tb olive oil, divided
1 tsp smoked paprika
1 shallot, diced
1 Tb brown rice flour
¼ tsp sea salt
cracked black pepper
¼ cup coconut cream
½ tsp horseradish
1 ripe avocado, diced
1 lemon, cut into wedges
2 Tb fresh parsley, chopped

1. Place the fish in a shallow baking pan and cover with the wine. Marinate in the refrigerator for at least an hour.
2. Preheat the oven to 400°F.
3. Drain the wine from the baking pan and drizzle one tablespoon of the olive oil on the snapper. Sprinkle with the paprika, salt, and pepper.
4. Bake for 15 minutes, or until fish is opaque and flakes easily.
5. Meanwhile prepare the sauce. Heat the remaining tablespoon oil in a small pot. Sautee the shallot until tender. Add the flour and cook for a minute before adding half a cup of water. Whisk to fully combine.
6. Remove the pot from the heat and stir in the coconut cream, horseradish, and avocado.
7. Squeeze the lemons over the fish, sprinkle with parsley, and serve with the avocado cream sauce.

Serves 4

Calories: 335
Fat: 16 grams
Sodium: 263 mg

Protein: 37 grams
Saturated Fat: 6 grams
Carbs: 8 grams

Sugar: 2 grams
Fiber: 3 grams

SHRIMP RISOTTO

This dish can easily be made vegan by substituting mushrooms for the shrimp.

2 tsp vegetable stock base, like Better than Bouillon
2 Tb olive oil
1 onion, chopped
2 garlic cloves, minced
½ tsp red pepper flakes
¼ cup parsley, chopped
1 lb cleaned shrimp
1 cup Arborio rice
½ cup dry white wine
1 lb asparagus, woody ends removed, cut into ½" pieces
1 Tb lemon juice
2 Tb nutritional yeast flakes

1. Heat four cups of water and white wine in a small pot. Add the vegetable stock base and stir until combined. Keep warm over very low heat.
2. Heat the oil in a large heavy pan. Add the onion, garlic, and red pepper flakes. Cook for five minutes.
3. Add the Arborio rice and stir for one minute. Slowly add the vegetable broth, half a cup at a time, stirring. Add each half cup only when the liquid in the rice pan has been almost completely absorbed.
4. When the rice is still al dente, after about fifteen minutes of cooking, add the asparagus. Five minutes later add the shrimp and parsley. Stir until the shrimp is fully cooked, about three minutes.
5. Remove from heat and add the lemon juice and yeast flakes.

Serves 4

Calories: 435   **Protein:** 32 grams   **Sugar:** 4 grams
Fat: 10 grams   **Saturated Fat:** 2 grams   **Fiber:** 8 grams
Sodium: 431 mg   **Carbs:** 48 grams

MUSSELS IN CURRY BROTH

Most curry pastes contain sugar and soybean oil, but A Taste of Thai doesn't. If soybean oil doesn't bother you, then Roland curry pastes are fine. The red and green pastes contain less sugar than the yellow. Do not eat any mussels that don't open during cooking.

2 lbs mussels
2 shallots, finely chopped
2 garlic cloves, minced
2 large tomatoes, diced
1 Tb coconut oil
1 Tb soy-free vegan margarine
1 can light coconut milk
2 Tb red curry paste
1 Tb lime juice
¼ cup cilantro leaves, chopped

1. Rinse the mussels. They should be tightly closed. Discard any that remain open as they are not alive and may have begun to spoil. Test open mussels by giving the shell a tap. Throw any away that don't close.
2. Heat the oil in a large soup pot or Dutch oven. Sauté the shallots and garlic for a few minutes until soft.
3. Add the tomatoes, margarine, coconut milk, and curry paste. Mix well and bring to a low boil.
4. Add the mussels, cover, and simmer until the mussels open, about four minutes.
5. Turn off heat, stir in the lime juice.
6. Serve the mussels in large, shallow bowls topped with the cooking broth and sprinkled with cilantro.

Serves 4

Calories: 330
Fat: 12 grams
Sodium: 472 mg
Protein: 35 grams
Saturated Fat: 4 grams
Carbs: 20 grams
Sugar: 6 grams
Fiber: 2 grams

SPICY GINGER MUSTARD SHRIMP

2 garlic cloves, crushed
1 Tb fresh ginger
1 tsp turmeric
1 tsp chili powder
1 tsp ground mustard powder
½ tsp ground coriander
1 Tb coconut oil
1 lb cleaned shrimp
¼ cup full-fat canned coconut milk
2 large tomatoes, diced
½ tsp sea salt

1. Heat the oil in a large pan. Add the spices (the first six ingredients) and cook, stirring, for two minutes.
2. Add the shrimp and coconut milk. Cook for another four or five minutes, until the shrimp are opaque.
3. Add the tomatoes and salt and cook for one or two more minutes until they are warm.
4. Serve over brown rice or mixed greens.

Serves 4

Calories: 200
Fat: 8 grams
Sodium: 496 mg

Protein: 24 grams
Saturated Fat: 6 grams
Carbs: 7 grams

Sugar: 3 grams
Fiber: 2 grams

10
DRINKS

Even individuals who care a great deal about what they put in their bodies like to have a tasty adult beverage every now and then. As long as you avoid added sugar and don't overdo it, it's okay to indulge in a drink every now and then.

MULLED WINE CIDER

A classic holiday drink. And a great way to use up the cheap bottles of red wine people bring to your holiday parties.

4 cups organic apple cider with no added sugar
rind of one orange
3 sticks of cinnamon
5 whole cloves
5 cardamom pods, crushed
10 whole peppercorns
1 bottle red wine

1. Combine everything except the wine in a large pot. Slowly bring to a boil and simmer for 20 minutes.
2. Add the red wine and return to a simmer.
3. Remove the solids from the pot and keep this warm over very low heat—it should no longer be simmering.

Makes seven 8oz servings

Calories: 160
Fat: 0 grams
Sodium: 11 mg

Protein: 0 grams
Saturated Fat: 0 grams
Carbs: 20 grams

Sugar: 14 grams
Fiber: 1 gram

WINTER WINE

A harder version of mulled wine—go light on this one!

750ml bottle red wine
¼ cup raw honey
rind of one orange
rind of one lemon
2 sticks of cinnamon
6 whole cloves
5 whole allspice
1 cup spiced rum or brandy
1 cup strong black tea

1. Combine everything except the rum and tea in a large pot. Slowly bring to a boil and simmer for 20 minutes.
2. Add the rum and tea and return to a simmer for 10 minutes.
3. Keep this warm over very low heat—it should no longer be simmering. Serve with extra cinnamon sticks.

Makes 10 4oz servings

Calories: 165   **Protein:** 0 grams   **Sugar:** 7 grams
Fat: 0 grams   **Saturated Fat:** 0 grams   **Fiber:** 1 gram
Sodium: 7 mg   **Carbs:** 11 grams

SUMMER WINE PUNCH

A light refreshing summer drink.

750ml bottle white or rosé wine, very cold
1 Tb raw honey
½ cup brandy
4 oz sliced strawberries
8 mint leaves, chopped
2 cups cold seltzer water
ice cubes

1. Combine everything except the ice and seltzer in a large pitcher. Chill in the refrigerator for at least half an hour to allow the flavors to mix.
2. Add the seltzer right before serving.
3. Serve over ice.

Makes 6 8oz servings

Calories: 145   **Protein:** 0 grams   **Sugar:** 4 grams
Fat: 0 grams   **Saturated Fat:** 0 grams **Fiber:** 0 grams
Sodium: 7 mg   **Carbs:** 6 grams

COQUITO

A vegan version of a traditional Puerto Rican holiday drink that normally contains egg and cream.

1 cup coconut water
1 14oz can full-fat coconut milk
2 cups unsweetened coconut milk
½ cup xylitol
2 tsp cinnamon
2 cups rum
1 Tb vanilla extract

1. Combine all ingredients in a blender.
2. Mix until combined.
3. Serve over ice.

Makes 10 6oz servings

Calories: 215   **Protein:** 1 gram   **Sugar:** 1 gram
Fat: 8 grams   **Saturated Fat:** 7 grams   **Fiber:** 1 gram
Sodium: 39 mg   **Carbs:** 9 grams

JAMAICAN SANGRIA

This provides a twist on the usual fruit and wine drink.

2 cups coconut water
1 cup coconut rum
1 cup pineapple juice, no sugar added
750 ml bottle white or rosé wine
8 oz fresh strawberries, sliced
1 small banana, halved and sliced
8 oz fresh or frozen blueberries
4 oz fresh or frozen mango, diced

1. Combine all ingredients in a large pitcher or serving bowl.
2. Mix until combined.
3. Chill for at least an hour.
4. Serve over ice.

Makes 9 8oz servings

Calories: 190
Fat: 0 grams
Sodium: 11 mg

Protein: 1 gram
Saturated Fat: 0 grams
Carbs: 18 grams

Sugar: 13 grams
Fiber: 2 grams

SPARKLING SUMMER SANGRIA

This version is lighter than the usual sangria. Feel free to try different fruits in this recipe.

2 cups watermelon, cut into ½" cubes
1 cup clear tequila
2 Tb raw honey
750 ml bottle sweet white wine
¼ cup lime juice
1 cup raspberries
4 cups seltzer

1. Combine all ingredients except the seltzer in a large pitcher or serving bowl.
2. Mix until combined.
3. Chill for at least an hour to allow the flavors to blend.
4. Add the seltzer right before serving.

Makes 12 8oz servings

Calories: 115   **Protein:** 0 grams   **Sugar:** 5 grams
Fat: 0 grams   **Saturated Fat:** 0 grams   **Fiber:** 1 gram
Sodium: 4 mg   **Carbs:** 8 grams

THE MORNING AFTER

This can help you if you indulged a bit too much the night before. It's also good for clearing the sinuses and taming upset stomachs.

6 cups water
⅓ cup lemon juice
3 whole garlic cloves, peeled
1 inch fresh ginger, chopped
¼ tsp cayenne
3 green tea bags

1. Combine all ingredients in a pot and bring to a boil.
2. Simmer for 20 minutes.
3. Remove the solids from the pot.
4. Sweeten with raw honey if you like.

Makes 5 8oz servings

Calories: 10   **Protein:** 0 grams   **Sugar:** 0 grams
Fat: 0 grams   **Saturated Fat:** 0 grams   **Fiber:** 0 grams
Sodium: 0 mg   **Carbs:** 3 grams

Made in the USA
Charleston, SC
22 March 2016